THE SACRED ART
OF
ANOINTING

Allison Stillman

Ojai, California

Copyright © 2008 by Allison Stillman

First Edition, 2008
Published by Romancing the Divine
347 North Poli Street Ojai, CA 93023
www.romancingthedivine.com

The author of this book does not dispense medical advice or prescribe any technique as a form of treatment for any physical, emotional, or medical problems without the advice of a physician. The intent of the author is only to offer information of a general nature to help in your search for emotional and spiritual well-being. The author and publisher assume no responsibility for any actions taken based upon this book.

Publisher's Cataloging-in-Publication

Stillman, Allison.
    The sacred art of anointing / Allison Stillman.
        p.   cm.

Includes bibliographical references.

LCCN 2008928562
    ISBN-13: 978-0-615-20922-7
    ISBN-10: 0-615-20922-X

    1. Essences and essential oils.   2. Spiritual life.   3. Self-actualization
    (Psychology)--Religious aspects.   I. Title.
    BF1442.E77S75   2008
    204'.4   QBI08-600149

Book design by Cindi Dietrich

Printed in the United States of America

*This book is dedicated to
my beloved friend, ally, and soul sister.*

*Diana, without you, this book would not exist.
I love you more than words.*

Note

This book is not meant to prescribe or treat any conditions or illness, nor is it meant to usurp any religious or spiritual powers, nor diminish the power of any religious organization or ceremony sanctified by them.

This book is intended as an informational guide only, any suggestions made are meant to supplement and not to be used as a substitute for professional medical care or treatment, nor religious structures and their organizations.

This book is an offering of spiritual techniques learned through the practice of anointing and are the opinions of the author based on the years of practice anointing people from all over the world, herself, her family and her loved ones, and the experiences of consistent anointing with consecrated essential oils.

Table of Contents

Acknowledgements

I would like to thank all of the friends, clients and loved ones who have helped me to birth this book into the world. You know who you are, and I hope you know how much I love you all!

My husband Michael, my devoted partner, thank you for walking this path with me, and being one of my strongest pillars of light.

My family of love, without you, none of this would have come to fruition, for you give me the unconditional love and support which creates the wind beneath my wings, and the power to dream the dream awake.

Cinderella, you are a fairy tale come true!!

All of my clients, you have been such gifts, and some of my best teachers, thank you for the love and support and knowing when it was your turn!

All of the teachers, masters and guides who work with me and through me, I am humbled, blessed and eternally grateful for the magnificence and guidance that you bring to me in every moment.

Introduction

Within each and every one of us, there exists a burning desire to "know thy self" or to know the deepest heart of ourselves, and many of us spend our lives trying to remember what we were born into this world knowing, that our inner landscape is primarily a Divine God/Goddess being, born to have the experience of life in a body. So we spend a good portion of our lives seeking to remember that deepest part of our truth, which takes us on a journey into spiritual traditions, religion and a general quest to find God and the deeper meaning of life.

I was born an inquisitive one and at once became a seeker. My curiosity grew as I did and evolved into an earnest quest for spiritual wisdom and knowledge. At the age of 7, I began to explore religion. My parents had come from diverse religious backgrounds and allowed us children to discover which religion called out the loudest and felt the truest for each of us.

I grew up in the South where there are churches on every corner and a vast amount of religion to choose from. So every Sunday, we would try out a different church, listen to a different service or sermon, learn about that particular brand of religion and try it on for size. I tried on each belief system with an earnest desire to align myself with religion and the Church.

As a child however, I knew even then, that God could not be contained within a church or a prescribed belief system, with the often times attached dogma and rules that look to contain God. I appreciated the faith that religion inspired, but I could never seem to reconcile all the prejudiced beliefs and limits that religion set upon God/Goddess.

I spent vast amounts of my childhood in the woods that surrounded our home, and have always been most at home in nature. I could hear the fairies and see the earth sprites dancing in the leaves and knew that nature was abundant with God, everywhere I looked God presented itself to me in the beauty and life that surrounded me while in nature. Anything so grand in design had to be filled with God's wonder and grace.

I believed then, and do firmly believe now, that God/Goddess, Great Mystery, The Supreme, Brahman, Allah, Divine Presence, or Spirit (there are many names to describe the same thing) is completely unlimited, and ultimately, in all things. Omnipotent, omnipresent, and omniscient are the words used to describe Divine Presence or God, in the Bible. In other words, God is all-powerful, having unlimited power and authority, is present in all places at the same time, and has infinite knowledge or a knowing of all things. The true meaning of that brings such an impact of understanding, and one which when I was a child, I fully understood to mean that everywhere I looked, including the mirror, there was, and is God.

The understanding of this as a child, allowed for a powerful connection to nature and in particularly, animals, plants, trees, flowers, and herbs. There was born within me an inherent sense of rooted-ness and connection to the Earth, and all Earth based traditions.

My paternal grandmother was born as an Omaha Indian, and from the time I can remember I have always had a very strong connection to the Native American based practices of honoring the Earth, adopting many traditions as part of my own practice.

My maternal grandmother was a horticulturist and some of the fondest memories from my childhood were with her in the wondrous garden she had created. We would pick peaches on warm summer days, and for me their was no grander feeling, than to have the sweet juice run down my face as I took my first bite of summer. She grew big bold roses with redolent perfumes, and the lush aromas would always tantalize my nose. These memories helped instill a passion for horticulture and fueled my quest for knowledge. In college I studied horticulture and botany and eventually got my landscape contractor's license.

My spiritual quest continued to evolve alongside my practical day-to-day life. I studied yoga, Buddhism, and more of the esoteric wisdom traditions. I attended my first yoga class when I was 16 years old, and at 19, I went to my first Buddhist meditation class, followed by a Sanskrit chanting class, and my spiritual odyssey blossomed into a much grander practice. I went to pow-wows, sweat lodges, and other Native American ceremonies, adopting many different cultures into my belief system and my daily devotional practice.

I left college and began a career, as a landscape contractor because I never wanted to be far from nature, for it too, was a meditation, and being in nature was my church. The Earth was, and continues to be for me, the Church of the Divine. The flowers, herbs, plants and trees always serve to tantalize my senses, and I have always had an inherent knowing that wellness on all levels can be achieved with the use of the plant kingdom.

As the years continued to pass, my path brought me to an enlightened spiritual master, Jose Luis Villanueva, a teacher who activated a much deeper awakening within me. I had the privilege to walk with this avatar for four years, and during this time, as I awakened deeply into consciousness, my vision and intuition began to open in a very profound way. On a number of occasions, my teacher would anoint our foreheads with perfumed oil before we went into meditation, and each time he would anoint me, I felt such a profound elevation of my Spirit. It was during this time, that my interest in plants and herbs led me to an earnest study of essential oils. Destiny once again led me to the next doorway.

My studies included many workshops, classes and books about essential oils, and in all my studies, there was never any mention of anointing, other than the traditional references and quotes from religious texts.

It was during a workshop almost twenty years ago, with the renowned aromatherapist and author Valerie Ann Worwood, that this book began its journey into the world. I had the grace and good fortune to be introduced to the pure essential oil of frankincense during that workshop, and upon inhaling deeply of the pungent aromatic elixir of the Gods and Goddesses; I was transported back into another time and place. I found myself at the foot of the cross, surrounded by pained expressions, that I knew at once to be the disciples. Before me, nailed to the cross was the master Jesus. The experience was so real; I could even smell the acrid dryness of the desert surroundings.

After what seemed to be but a few moments time, I found myself fully present in the classroom with many eyes focused upon me. The woman seated next to me asked, "What happened to you, are you all right?"

My response was without thought, "I want to do anointing work."

She looked at me puzzled, and asked, "What is that?"

I looked back at her even more puzzled, and said, "I have absolutely no idea, in fact, I don't even know why I said that."

Class resumed and from that day forward, I began to practice my meditation after anointing myself first with frankincense oil. I would apply the oil to my crown chakra, my third eye, and inhale deeply of the rich, woody, and deeply intoxicating essence of frankincense.

Frankincense has among its physical properties the ability to calm one's breath, which assists with its ability to elevate one into spiritual and meditative states. I've even had numerous clients who have experienced hallucinatory states when inhaling frankincense.

Because of this inherent ability to induce meditative states, frankincense has been used for thousands of years in religious and spiritual ceremonies around the world. And to this day, some of the Catholic Churches still use frankincense oil to anoint during Baptismal ceremonies, one of the seven sacraments offered by the Church. A study of most spiritual traditions will find the use of fragrance from plants used to induce states of meditation, whether through the use of anointing, the burning of incense, or the diffusing of essential oils.

As I continued to use the frankincense oil with my meditations, I began to notice my intuitive vision becoming deeply enhanced, and commenced seeing a reoccurring picture of the temples in Egypt thousands of years ago. Over and over again, I would find myself inside one of the temples, which was home to the priestess, and I would be allowed to watch the ancient ceremony of anointing that was performed there. Each vision in my meditation revealed more details about anointing and after 6 months of these visions, while on a meditation retreat with my teacher Jose Luis, my closest friend and dear sister, revealed to me that she too, had been having many of the same visions. We both realized that we were being given a great gift of healing and awakening from another time and place.

I became fascinated and eager to learn more. My thirst for written information about anointing led me to local libraries, rare manuscript libraries, Gnostic archive galleries, searches in old bookstores, and all through the Internet. I began to realize that anointing dates back to a time when we all sought out and lived a much more spiritual lifestyle, and was practiced in many different spiritual traditions throughout history. Anointing was practiced to consecrate our selves to the sacred and Divine. To my dismay however, there was no practical information written about anointing, only references to the inherent power of anointing found within religious texts, such as the Bible.

So my dear friend and I began to practice on each other, and then on many of our loved ones. We watched as miraculous healings occurred, and the most transformational experiences happened over and over to people right before our very eyes. And so it was that the inspiration for this book began.

My beliefs about anointing are based on years of practicing and teaching this ancient art across the country and watching the profound transformational effects of anointing. I have come to know the many truths I share here in this book about anointing with practiced certainty. I have watched over the years, as the people who have come for sessions have been completely transformed by the experience, and I have realized that anointing is a tool to connect us with our God-like state, our Divine inner nature. Anointing has the power to clear away old limiting belief systems, acquired as identification during childhood, in the womb, or throughout our lives, and genetic patterns that no longer serve us, or might stand in the way of the recognition of our sacred Divine nature.

I have come to see anointing as a tool of Divine activation, and the people who have come over the years to be anointed are always at a point of passage in their lives. Anointing is a powerful rite of passage that enables people to let go of the old and initiate a whole new way of being. It is also an incredible tool to align, balance and integrate the body, mind and Spirit.

Anointing with essential oils has assisted me in consecrating the very nature of my truth, as a Divine being, walking the human journey. Anointing has become an essential part of daily living for me, and I can't even imagine life without it. I am more focused, more balanced, more spiritually centered, and more willing to live life passionately as a result of my own daily anointing. My desire to write this book was born out of a wish to share the magic of this ancient art.

This book contains information about the history of anointing and the practical application of essential oils for the ceremony of anointing. It also contains information about crystals and gemstones, energy work, and sound therapy to assist the application of the essential oils in raising one's consciousness, to help bring the body into alignment, balance, and radiant health, and help heal the heart, emotions, and mind, and to activate higher states of awareness. In addition, there are practical ceremonies at the end of each chapter that will allow the reader to practice using essential oils to anoint themselves and others.

Anointing has been an incredible gift and a tool that has fostered a romance with the deepest part of my divinity, and cultivated a strong, healthy constitution, and a happy, joyful heart. Allow me to share it with you...

Chapter 1

The Ancient Art of Anointing

More over the Lord spoke unto Moses saying:

Take thou unto thee principal spices of pure myrrh...

of sweet cinnamon... of sweet calamus...

of cassia... and of olive...

and thou shalt make it an oil of holy ointment,

an ointment compound after the art of the apothecary:

it shall be an holy anointing oil.

Exodus 30:20-25

Anoint
To apply oil as a sacred rite, especially for consecration.

Consecrate
To devote to a purpose with deep solemnity, or dedication;
to make or declare sacred.

Sacred
Entitled to veneration by association with divinity.

Divine
Of, pertaining to, or proceeding from a god, especially
the Supreme Being (love); supremely good, heavenly, god-like.

Today there is a growing awareness on the planet seeming to indicate a grand spiritual evolution occurring amongst us. We are awakening to the remembrance of the Divine, God/Goddess, or Spirit that resides *within* each and every one of us. As it says in the Bible, God (Spirit) is omnipotent, omnipresent, and omniscient, which in essence means that Spirit is unfailing, rich, lavish, abundant and completely unlimited, everywhere and all powerful and abides within each one of us.

Therefore, God/Goddess/Spirit/the Divine exists in all beings, all things, and is the source of all creation and completely uncontainable. Within this knowledge comes the freedom we all seek, the reclamation of our selves as Spirit, as God/Goddess, as Divine and Supreme.

Quantum physicists are now beginning to prove this ancient spiritual teaching, and have even identified and photographed an electromagnetic field that exists everywhere and is in all things. Gregg Braden has called this unified field, "The Living Mind of God". This "Living Mind of God" extends everywhere and exists in all things including each and every one of us.

Anointing with consecrated essential oils is a tool that each of us can offer to our selves and to our loved ones as a path of remembrance to the truth of who we really are, that of Divine creatures. Anytime we seek to remember the truth of who we really are, anointing with essential oils will support our intention in finding Spirit in the body. Anointing, whether a simple ceremony, or the more complex ceremonies of the Egyptian priestesses, will assist in the sacred declaration and consecration of our selves as holy vessels or temples of the Divine.

Anointing heralds back as one of the oldest, and most traditional uses for essential oils. Recorded history traces this use of essential oils back more than 6,000 years. Although the actual ceremony or substance employed in anointing could vary greatly from one culture unto another, we find it nearly universal in the vast history of religion. There are more than 155 references to anointing found within the Bible alone, and it is within this context that we see the greatest written historical evidence of the reverence held for the rite or ceremony of anointing.

Anointing with essential oils has been used for thousands of years as a method of consecration for our selves, our altars, temples, and homes to the service and devotion of the Divine, to symbolize and assure the presence and the pleasure of the Divine in a holy place.

**Take the anointing oil and anoint
the tabernacle and everything in it.
Consecrate it and all its furnishings, and it will be holy.**
Exodus 40:9-10

**Then shalt thou take the anointing oil
and pour it upon his head, and anoint him.**
Exodus 29:7

Anointing, as described in the Bible, dedicates one to the service of the Divine, and so facilitates the consecration of one as a vessel of the Divine.

Anointing oils have traditionally been specific blends of consecrated essential oils known for their exalted spiritual proper-ties, and their ability to lift us into higher states of awareness and consciousness. Essential oils are the subtle, volatile liquids, the complete essence or soul of plants, flowers, trees, roots, and seeds extracted through precise methods of distillation.

Since as early as 4,000 BC, humans have used the oils from macerated plants for healing, for visionary, religious and spiritual ceremony, to scent or perfume, and for beauty preparations.

We find evidence of this worldwide in many of the museums displaying artifacts of ancient cultures. In the British Museum, there are a number of antique Egyptian jars and bottles dating between 3,000 and 2,000 BC that verify the use of essential oils within the Egyptian culture.

There are many hieroglyphics inscribed upon the Egyptian temple walls depicting the ceremonies performed involving the use of essential oils. When the tomb of Tutankhamen was opened in 1922, a number of alabaster jars were found buried with the many treasures. These jars, placed in the tomb more than 3,000 years ago, were found to contain unguents which when tested revealed the presence of frankincense and spikenard, two of the more holy and sacred essential oils to the ancient Egyptians. And in fact, carved on the back of King Tut's throne, is a golden inlay depicting King Tut being anointed by his mother, the Queen, believed to have been Kiya.

There are many tablets, papyrus, and hieroglyphics that have been translated to show that the use of essential oils is well documented within many ancient civilizations. A clay tablet was discovered in Syria in 1973 that held the first written formula for plant remedies and is believed to have been created in Sumeria, 4,000 BC, describing the use of fennel, galbanum, and pine. Another clay tablet dating back to about 1,800 BC, from the Sumerian and Babylonian regions, revealed an order for the import of the essential oils of cedar, myrrh, and cypress. These particular tablets would seem to support the idea that knowledge and appreciation of essential oils was very evident 4-6,000 years ago within these cultures.

In January of 1997, an article in the Los Angeles Times reported that an ancient frankincense trade route had been discovered by a team of archeologists, which unearthed a wealth of discoveries. The trail begins in the recently discovered city of Ubar in Oman, and leads into the Middle East, again affirming the fact that frankincense was highly valued and traded in the world.

Frankincense is the dried resin harvested from a shrub that grows well only in the Qara Mountains of Oman. At various times throughout history, frankincense has been deemed more precious than gold, due to its use in religious ceremonies for the consecration of temples and holy ones, and in the treatment of illness. It was also highly valued for its ability to take one into meditative states and altered states of consciousness. The world is well acquainted with the gifts from the Three Wise Men of frankincense, gold and myrrh, which were given to the baby Jesus, as he lay newly born in the manger. There are vast amounts of information available about the historical use of essential oils throughout different civilizations of the world; however, it is the perfume industry that is responsible for the greatest rise in the awareness of essential oils in today's world. But in terms of significance, it is the religious and spiritual use of essential oils that are responsible for bringing oils their greatest premium. This extensive *spiritual* use of essential oils validates their ability to elevate consciousness. Anointing with essential oils is one of the most powerful tools available to us today in our reclamation of Spirit, to make or declare our selves sacred and Divine.

It was within the Egyptian culture that anointing made its most significant impact. The ancient Egyptians were very adept in their alchemical knowledge about, and use of, essential oils, and the ceremony of anointing with essential oils was practiced to honor all great rites of passage. Baptism, Confirmation, Communion, Ordination, marriage, and death were all celebrated with rites or ceremonies of anointing. The Egyptian's ceremony of anointing was an elaborate structure involving the use of essential oils, sound and color therapies, vibrational healing, and energy work (i.e., reiki), fasting and meditation. With the practice of anointing, the Egyptians were able to activate profound transformational shifts within the body, mind and spirit.

The temple of Dendarah, along the river Nile, was home to the priestess. Dendarah was a temple devoted to the order of the priestess, as the temple of Edfu was home to the priest. The priestess was initiated into the more esoteric teachings of the ancient Egyptian mysteries and ceremonies. Anointing was a powerful ceremony that all priestesses were taught as their working alchemical knowledge of essential oils was developed. The main thrust of the priestesses instruction was focused on the specific properties of essential oils, their ability to assist with healing and their inherent ability to ordain one into the state of awareness as Supreme Being or Divine. It has been said by some that it was the temple of Dendarah where Jesus was introduced to essential oils and their ability to heal, during his time of exodus.

The temple of Dendarah seems to have the most evidence of the ceremony of anointing validated by the inscriptions carved upon the temple walls depicting the use of essential oils in ceremony. It is clearly evident that this temple was a place where people would come to reclaim themselves as Divine, and to honor all great rites of passage.

The anointing ceremonies practiced by the priestesses in the temples were a more elaborate system of anointing, and more inclusive of other tools and modalities that were an assurance of an activation of the soul's awareness and evolution, particularly when used in combination with the sacred essential oils.

People came to be initiated by the priestess and underwent many days of preparation, fasting, and remaining in silence and meditation to prepare them selves for the ceremony of anointing. Many of our modern day religious rites are loosely based on this ancient wisdom and on the anointing ceremonies practiced within the temples of our ancestors.

In the ancient Egyptian civilizations, we were a more spiritually oriented society. Anointing played a significant role in our daily lives, in addition to the more complex rites performed in the temples. Within many of our homes or temples, we held vessels of essential oils, and would anoint our selves daily. We had anointing jars that sat by our doorway, dispensing the oils of frankincense, lavender and chamomile, specifically blended for the well-known protective qualities these oils afford.

We would anoint our selves in order to cleanse and reinforce our auras, or the energetic fields around our body, raising our vibration and dispelling negative energies upon entrance into the home. Each day we would dispense a few drops of the aromatic elixir and anoint the crown of our head, our forehead or "third eye," the shoulders, solar plexus, the palms of our hands, and the soles of our feet. We would summon the assistance of our Guardian angels and masters to strengthen the intention of our anointing, and we would leave and enter the home or temple as consecrated, sacred vessels of the Divine protected while outside in the world from negative influences and energies.

In an attempt to validate my belief that essential oils have the ability to alter our etheric body, or our energetic body, I engaged a very good friend of mine, Pamala Oslie in an experiment to see just how the application of essential oils affected the auric field of the human body. Pamala, who is an internationally well known psychic and author and has written her own books called "Life

Colors", "Love Colors" and "Make Your Dreams Come True", has the intuitive ability to actually see the colors of the aura. She watched my aura as I applied and inhaled several different essential oils. With the application of frankincense, my aura colors brightened immeasurably, while the application of rose oil, brought a soft hue of pink into my aura. The application of a blend of different sacred oils, including frankincense, rose, lavender, and lotus created magic, and actually turned my aura gold. Pamala said, "I have never seen gold in anyone's aura before, the only time I have seen gold in an aura has been when I have looked at pictures of Jesus or Buddha."

This experience validated my belief that the essential oils have the ability to change and clear the energy around our bodies. With our auras cleared and balanced it is much easier for the body, mind and spirit to come into alignment, and move us into higher states of awareness, or affect healing within the body.

According to ancient Egyptian wisdom, when a loved one was experiencing any difficulty, we would anoint them as a subtle recall to the remembrance of the true nature of who we really are beneath the surface façade of our personalities, and to restore balance and equilibrium to the body, mind and spirit. Whenever we would come together as husband and wife in the act of Communion, we anointed our selves with the more sensual oils of rose, myrrh, and sandalwood before the conjoining, to elevate the act into an ecstatic expression of spiritual reunion and loving.

Thousands of years ago in Egypt, we all recognized our true spiritual nature as Divine, and within that knowledge came the freedom to practice anointing. As we begin to remember once again our spiritual heritage, we are able to recognize the gifts that assist us in centering in the truth of our spirit, and remembering our Divine nature. Anointing creates a passionate romance with Divinity, and is a tool to help keep us resonating at a healthy, balanced electromagnetic, or vibrational frequency.

Anointing ceremonies were practiced in the home and temples until the advent of the Christian revolution. Around the same time that Jesus lived in a human body, Christianity began to take preference as a belief system and the prescription of a one-god theory began to infiltrate mass consciousness. It was during this time that some of the practices used to perpetuate spirituality and healing began to come under suspicion.

With the onset of the 11th century, the first tribunals were formed with the intention of abolishing heretics or anyone who maintained opinions contrary to those of the Church. The Inquisition, as this tribunal came to be known, began an earnest hunt for all those accused of practicing any form of alchemy or healing with herbs, plants, and essential oils when not sanctioned by the Church. The Inquisition trials were notoriously cruel and often torture was used as a means of procuring confessions from the accused. Once the confession was obtained, the accused was convicted and sentenced. The sentence was generally one of three prescribed methods of death, stoning, drowning, or the most widely recognized method of burning. Millions of women were burned at the stake, accused and condemned as witches, while trying only to help heal the sick and dying.

Anointing was recognized by the Church as a powerful means to invoke the presence of God or the Supreme, and would often produce miraculous healing effects. The right to anoint was revoked from the masses and claimed the sole right of the Church for the consecration and salvation of the Divine. Using this powerful ploy to gain control of the masses, God/Goddess, the Divine became accessible only through the Church. All memory of the practice and knowledge of anointing was suppressed and eventually lost within the lay people. The various Inquisitions and tribunals were not fully abolished in Europe until the early 1800's, and it is only recently that systems of healing and consecration have begun to have their renaissance on the planet as the fear of retribution was far too great to attempt practicing until now.

Anointing is a powerful tool to reconstitute our connection to God and the Supreme, and once again we are able to take responsibility for our own spiritual growth, practice, and renewal without the fear of punishment when practiced outside the sanctity of a Church.

The recorded history of anointing (of which there is scant written information) demonstrates the fact that anointing ceremonies can vary greatly. One can be anointed with a single drop of oil, drops of blessed holy water, alchemically created blends of oils, gemstones, sacred sound tones, or color rays. Together with intention, anointing can be a powerful tool to awaken Spirit.

Move into the temple of the Divine, and ask each House, or chakra (a Sanskrit word to describe an energy center, or spinning wheel of the body) within your temple (body), to remember, to balance, align, integrate and activate within Spirit.

As we dance throughout each House (a term coined to represent the chakra) in our body temples, ignite Divinity along the way and awaken from the slumber of forgetfulness into a vital, conscious vessel of God and Goddess. Anointing will activate the stir from slumber into a vibrancy of life and love.

Now I know that the Lord saves his anointed; he answers from his holy heaven with the saving power of his right hand.
Psalms 20:6

But you have an anointing from the Holy One, and all of you know the truth.
John 2:20

Allow the power of anointing to awaken a Divine presence and inspire the continued evolution we all so desperately seek.

Just as humanity has evolved throughout time, so has the rest of Earth's treasures, specifically, the plant kingdom. The consciousness of the plant world continues to evolve, maintaining a memory of its vast history throughout time. The essential oils derived from the plant through the art of proper distillation retain the consciousness of that plant and its vast use throughout the history of our evolution. The live molecular energy of each plant can be maintained through very precise distillation methods. It is here that the soul essence of the plant resides. Essential oils are crystalline structures that carry light, and are electromagnetic, as we ourselves are. They vibrate and cause selective synchronous vibration when applied to the body, not only affecting the physical body, but also the emotional and mental bodies as well. Meaning, they have the ability to create a similar electromagnetic vibration when applied to the body, affecting the physical, mental, emotional, and spiritual well-being.

As Richard Thompson says in "The Brain, A Neuroscience Primer, "The similarity of the genetic material in all forms of life that exist in the world today, including bacteria, plants, animals, and people, indicates that all living organisms descended from the same single cell-line." In other words, plants and people are from

10

the same familial line and as such have a very strong connection, which is one of the reasons that essential oils have the ability to affect us and change our electromagnetic frequency or vibration. Simply put, essential oils have the ability to lift our vibration, which is how they assist us in moving into higher states of awareness and consciousness.

With that understanding, it's easy to see why essential oils have been used for thousands of years in religious and spiritual ceremony to initiate one into a remembrance of Divine Spirit. There is a level of remembrance within the consciousness of the oils themselves, more specifically, to the living consciousness of the plants that is also holy and sacred. Essential oils carry a memory of their role as anointing oils or "chrism". Chrism derives its name from the Greek word chrismata, which means anointing.

Throughout many of the ancient, sacred, and religious texts, chrism or anointing oils are spoken of again and again. Saint Cyril of Jerusalem explains, *"It is with such oil that Christians are anointed and become a "Royal People," imbued and dressed with a Christ-like essence. Take care not to imagine that this chrism is anything ordinary, but the divinely conferred gift of the power of Christ, made efficacious of Holy Spirit by the presence of Divinity."*

Sacred scriptures further clarify the significance of these oils as the very essence and presence of Christ,

Your name is ointment poured upon me.

Canticle 1:3

In an anointing rite, we effectively become clothed again with Christ, and with Divine Presence and Grace. We become a new "Christos," the Greek word for "The Anointed One." The Divine Spirit of Christ *is* this chrism, this sweet anointing ointment, and the mystical and spirit-filled presence of God/Goddess, infused in essential oils.

It is this ancient, sacred memory and soul consciousness, which is alive and present in essential oils today. The gift of anointing with essential oils as in a sacramental rite of Baptism, Confirmation, or assisting the dying becomes incredibly powerful and Christ invoking when performed with the precious anointing oils. Anointing with essential oils or chrism, allows the essence of

Divine Spirit, grace, and love, to bathe and fill the individual.

Throughout time, anointing has assisted humanity in healing and elevating seekers into Divine states of ecstatic consciousness, allowing for re-union with Spirit, and a return into the heart of the Christos.

One's spiritual development, growth, maturation, and fortification can only come about by a consistent exposure to, and unified experience of Divine Spirit. By proclaiming our desire to stay in, or return to Divine unification with the anointing of essential oils, this Christ-like chrism sanctifies us as holy and allows for complete immersion into Divinity.

The spirit of the Lord is upon me,
because he has anointed me with oil...

Isaiah 61:1

In any anointing ceremony or rite, using consecrated oils or chrism effectuates the mystical presence of Holy Spirit. To consecrate essential oils requires the intention of invoking the Divine into the vessel of oils specifically blended for each sacrament or ceremony. The invocation can be simple or a ceremony can be created around the blending of the oils. This blessing, or consecration of the anointing oils should include holding the oils between one's palms and invoking a clear, gracious invitation for the presence of Divine Spirit to be made manifest into the blessed chrism.

When we anoint our selves and our loved ones on a daily basis, we are actualizing a remembrance, a re-union and fortification with the Divine.

Anointing oils are used to seal, consecrate, validate and establish the presence of Divinity upon those whom the mark of anointing has been placed.

And the Lord said unto him, go through the city
of Jerusalem and set a mark upon the foreheads

Ezekiel 9:4-6

And so it happens that the anointed ones become participants in the nature of Divinity.

Our desire to be enmeshed in the nature of our Divinity can indeed be greatly supported, enhanced and assured with the anointing of holy oils. Essential oils carry this inherent responsibility within the very essence of their nature, and have grown and evolved to become even more powerful in their ability to consecrate us as Divine.

There are no rules or limits when it comes to devising a ceremony or practice of anointing. Carolyn Myss, in her book "Why People Don't Heal" did a brilliant comparison of the seven energy centers to the seven sacraments. We can create anointing ceremonies to correspond with each of these sacraments and honor specific growth cycles within our lives. And we can also create anointing ceremonies to honor each House within our body. The word House symbolizes the complexity of a home, its various rooms, feelings, emotions, and the various aspects of all the occupants that reside there.

In the following chapters, there are suggestions and comparisons for specific anointing ceremonies, and in addition, ceremonies created to correlate to some of the Christian sacraments and the corresponding Houses. There is also information about essential oils, their properties and effects, and information about the energy centers of the body, or Houses, that relate to specific parts of the body, food types, sounds, crystals and gemstones, as well as ceremonies for keeping each House balanced. As we maintain balance within the body, mind and spirit, our lives become healthy, radiant, joy-filled and abundantly graceful. Anointing is a glorious gift that we can easily give to ourselves, and all of our loved ones.

In this glorified realm of human existence, one of the greatest tools available to reconstitute our Divine connection remains the art of anointing.

Chapter 2

Sacred Scents

Essential Oils... *what are they?*

Most evolved plants go through a transformation
from the primitive germ, to the exuberance of the
flower in a natural movement towards spirituality.....
where the flower in its impermanence and openness,
represents an instant of rapture and jubilation.

Goethe

Essential oils are the aromatic and volatile, liquid substances that are composed of crystalline structures imbued with light and are found in plants: flowers, trees, herbs, roots, grasses, and seeds. The wide variety of aromatic oils obtained from the plant kingdom, have been described as the hormones or the "life-blood" of a plant. This highly concentrated essential nature of the plant, or essential oil, is responsible for the transpiration and life processes of the plant, carrying messages and frequencies of change to the plant, e.g. when to flower, when to go to seed, and also give the plant the ability to know when to heal. These oily, volatile compounds are the basis of plant scents and are either end products or by-products of plant metabolism. These oily compounds are stored in special glands or organs within the plant and are released most commonly through the process of steam distillation.

The science of distillation is complex and covered in other books extensively, but the basic art goes something like this. Depending upon the plant and the location of the essential oil, e.g. rose and jasmine store the essential oils in the flowers of the plant, in geranium and peppermint the oil is stored in the leaves. The plant material is harvested and placed inside a metal or glass vat, which then gets heated to a specific temperature with an exact time and pressure dependent upon the plant. The heat releases steam infused with plant material, which then passes through a condenser and the resultant liquid gets deposited into a vessel. When the liquid cools, the oil floats to the top and is then skimmed off the top and collected as the essential oil.

The remaining water is called a hydrosol and contains minute traces of the compounds of the plant and can be used quite success-fully for applications that require more dilute concentrations of the chemical compounds found in the essential oil. It is important that the plant matter is grown organically to avoid the concentra-tion of pesticides in the oil.

The role of essential oils are very evident when we walk through a rose garden in full bloom on a hot summer day and smell the sweet fragrance of the flowers, or crush lavender flowers between our fingertips and feel the oily, sweet release of the oils, or peel a warm orange picked fresh from the tree and watch as the essential oil droplets disperse into the air in a fragrant rush of jubilation and sweet, fruity perfume.

The history of aromatherapy dates back thousands of years, even though the word aromatherapy only came into being in the early 20th century when a scientist named Maurice Gattefosse coined the word. The word aromatherapy means a therapy using only the aromas (i.e. essential oils) of plants, and not the plants in their entirety (i.e. herbalism).

Back in 1920, Gattefosse was a French cosmetic chemist working in his laboratory when he had an accident that resulted in a severe burn on his arm. There was a vat on his workbench and intending to cool down the burn, he immersed his arm in the vat, thinking it to be cool water. The vat turned out to be a container of fresh lavender essential oil that his colleague had placed on the workbench. He was amazed as the burning sensation began to decrease and then stop within just a few minutes. He continued to work with the lavender oil and to his surprise, the burn healed without a trace of a scar. He then analyzed the properties of the essential oil and recognized many chemical constituents that were responsible for the healing. Thus began the re-emergence of the ancient art of aromatherapy into the modern world.

It is not clear as to whether the extraction and use of aromatic material began in Egypt or India, but there is evidence that both cultures practiced extraction and the use of essential oils in their daily lives, for religious and mystical practices, for medicinal practices and to preserve the dead. It is believed that the primitive start of distillation involved using animal fat to soak the plant material and then wool cloth was added, which was allowed to soak in the mixture. The cloth was then burned off and the oil droplets were released and then collected, to be used for the various properties found within the plants in a more concentrated form.

There is further evidence that not only were the Egyptians and Indians using aromatics, but the Assyrians, Babylonians, Phoenicians, Jews, Chinese, Greeks, Romans, and eventually the Christians, all burned resins of plants in religious and mystical ceremonies. There are even indications that the use of plants may actually date back 18,000 years, as there are cave paintings depicting the use of plants for healing purposes found in the Dordogne region. What is most evident is that all cultures in one form or another have used plant-based materials for healing and spiritual ceremony, and we can learn a great deal from our ancestors.

This is the story of an eternal relationship. A relationship that extends beyond the limitation of time and species, a friendship of sisters, brothers, lovers, and family; the family of essential oils and our relationships with them. Here we find trees, shrubs, herbs, flowers, seeds, leaves, roots and shoots all lending their heart and souls, their spirit, in the form of herbs and essential oils, so that they may assist our walk into health and well-being.

Essential oils are derived through many different methods of extraction, the most popular method being that of steam distillation, which when performed to the exacting formula specific to each individual plant, maintains the live molecules of the plant. Lavender for example must be distilled in vats smaller than two thousand liters, with temperatures close to 185 degrees for no less than one and a half hours, with zero pounds of pressure to maintain the live molecules of the plant. Those live molecules all contain an electromagnetic frequency, a measurable unit of energy, and are the same energy that exists in all of nature, including the human species.

Essential oils carry messages and frequencies of change to the plant, when to flower, when to seed, when to grow, when to reproduce, what color of flower to produce, how to heal a wound, or recover from freezing temperatures, and inevitably when to die.

Essential oils seem to function on a similar level within the human body, mind and spirit, once they are absorbed either by inhalation or through absorption of the skin, blood and tissues of the body.

Essential oils have been used for thousands of years in the healing and alignment of the body, mind, and spirit. They are powerful tools to help activate and awaken spiritual evolution and consciousness. The oils serve to remind us that we have, plants, animals and people all, traveled together since the beginning of time, each species evolving and expanding through time.

As living species, plants, animals and human, we all contain energy. As such, we all emit electromagnetic energy, sometimes referred to as an aura, or halo, and which can actually be measured and photographed with specific Kirilian cameras. There has been research done using Kirilian cameras to monitor the aura and the changes in the aura with the application of essential oils. These photos show that the application of essential oils will actually change the colors within the aura.

The essential oil of a plant is capable of making the plant's aura visible as well. Walk out into a lavender field on a hot summer day, inhale the sweet, clean, floral fragrance of the plants and hold your face up close, looking toward the sun, and you will see the aura of the lavender. The actual essential oil droplets are dispersed into the air above the plant by the heat, and are visible to the naked eye.

It is also the essential oil that creates the fragrance in a flower. Behold the rose, a symbol of love throughout the history of time. If you ever find yourself in a garden where old fashioned roses are in full bloom, stand in front of one, and glory in the vibrant color, allowing that color to stimulate you, knowing that essential oils dictated the exact hues and tones of the color in that flower. Then allow yourself to inhale deeply of the intoxicating fragrance (note: new hybridized types of roses are not all graced with a strong fragrance. In fact, most of the truly fragrant roses are older types of roses), and know also, that it is the essential oil in the plant and its flowers that is responsible for the fragrance of the rose.

The delicious sweet floral notes of rose have been known throughout time as an aphrodisiac, which could account for its high demand in the perfume industry. Roses have long been the symbol of love, and the essential oil has an evocative ability to draw one into a state of love. It's no wonder that rose oil carries one of the highest electrical frequencies and is also one of the most expensive essential oils. Just standing in the middle of a rose garden can be quite a transformative experience, and essential oils play a big role in that experience.

Standing at the foot of an ancient tree, we feel majesty, wisdom, strength and solidity. We sense a strong, rooted connection to the Earth. It is, once again, the essential oil that is the lifeblood of the tree, directing the trees to become their glorious stately presence.

The ancient trees, having lived since the beginning of time, have genetically inherited much wisdom and obtained information through the morphogenetic evolutionary fields of life.

The magnificent elders are here to infuse us with their strength and wisdom. The concentration of this energy in an essential oil assists in raising our frequency into that of the ancient wisdom keepers, the trees. In addition to the important task of sequestering carbon, the essential oils of the trees are valuable tools for healing.

Perhaps, an understanding of this will help bring a new sense of urgency to our protection of the old growth forests all over the world. The old trees contain all of the secrets garnered since the beginning of time, and can affect healing on many levels. Many of the tree oils have very powerful healing properties as well. Cedarwood for example, is antiseptic, anti-seborrheic, astringent, diuretic, expectorant, anti-fungal, a nerve sedative, and circulatory stimulant.

Every essential oil available to us, affects each aspect of our being, the physical, emotional, mental and spiritual. Therein lies the true mystery of essential oils. They invite us to come and experience a dance of discovery, exploring each component of them, and their effects on our well-being.

Essential oils are so complex, the complete mystery of their magic, remains unsolved. What we do know about the science of essential oils is that they are a mixture of organic compounds such as ketones, terpenes, esters, alcohotes, and hundreds of other molecules, with many being too small for classification.

How they work, is much easier to understand. Because the molecules are so small, they penetrate the skin and enter the blood, tissues and organs. Scientists have witnessed that essential oils tend to gather in a specific part of the body time and again, which determines their therapeutic value and uniqueness.

It is from the use of essential oils that modern medicine has evolved. Aspirin, made of salicylic acid extracted from the willow tree, is an example. The essential oil Melalueca, or tea tree oil, is a powerful anti-viral, anti-bacterial, and anti-fungal, and is ten times as strong as carbolic acid.

The more the properties of plants and oils are explored and researched, the more we realize that every plant is here for a reason, and all plants will lend themselves to humanity for healing. True essential oils all contain anti-viral, anti-fungal, and anti-bacterial properties, but many may also contain anti-inflammatory, antidepressant, analgesic, antibiotic, antiseptic, anti-microbial, anti-spasmodic, anti-tumoral, and the list goes on and on. Essential oils also contain hormones, vitamins, enzymes and minerals, every ingredient to keep a plant, flower, or tree in perfect health.

With the advent of super bugs, viruses and bacteria and their developing resistance to man-made medicines (antibiotics), we may really want to explore nature's apothecary, and the healing properties of essential oils.

Back in 1992 Bruce Tainio, of Tainio Technologies, an independent division of Eastern State University in Washington began testing the electrical frequency of essential oils, using a very sophisticated machine capable of measuring kilohertz, or units of energy. This research showed that within 21 minutes of an application of essential oils to the feet, the frequencies of the body were raised measurably. He discovered that the human body in a healthy state vibrates within the range of 52-75 kilohertz. Whenever we stress the body, lack of sleep, poor diet, smoking, drinking, etc., our frequency drops, and we allow the frequency of illness, which is a much lower frequency, (below 40), to influence us.

Along with Gary Young, the founder of Young Living Essential Oils, they discovered that the application of essential oils to the feet of the body would actually change the electrical frequency of certain organs in the body. Although they were unable to get consistent numbers to validate their testing, there was indeed a change made to the body and the electrical frequency with each application of therapeutic grade essential oils. From years of practical application my experience tells me that there is great truth to their studies and I truly believe that the continued application of therapeutic grade essential oils can help us maintain a higher state of frequency in the body, or return the body to a higher electromagnetic frequency, and stay above the state of disease.

There have been vast amounts of study done on the affects of fragrance on the limbic system, and how the body is affected through the sense of smell.

The Olfactory Research Fund has financed research for the last 25 years into the study of the positive effects of fragrance on human behavior. Research findings have proven that fragrances can successfully reduce stress and anxiety, increase alertness and performance, and have a beneficial effect on sleep patterns. Fragrance is now being used in airports, hospitals, hotels, schools, factories, corporate offices, hospitals and nursing homes for the purpose of creating environments that are conducive to relaxation, learning, increased performance, alertness, and healing.

The inhalation of fragrance will quickly transport one into memories, images and feelings, and the use of fragrance is one of the most exciting arenas of research in the psychotherapeutic worlds. Sigmund Freud concluded in one of his studies, that the repression of smell is a leading cause of mental illness.

The impulse of smell has an extraordinary ability to bypass the neo-cortex of the brain, or intellect and move directly into the limbic system. The limbic system is the part of the brain responsible for behavior. Although much is still unknown, we do know that the limbic system does influence the intuition, emotions, creativity, hunger, thirst, sexual desire and more. The power of smell has the ability to influence us in many ways.

The inhalation of frankincense oil has a direct effect on the hypothalamic region, which also stimulates the release of hormones and messages to the entire endocrine system, eliciting bodily behaviors. Frankincense has been known to stimulate the release of serotonin, the hormone responsible for taking us into relaxed states of bliss, and deep meditation, hence its popularity for spiritual and religious ceremony throughout time.

The synchronization of menstrual periods amongst women, who are close or live together, is traced to the release of pheromones from the body, another behavior stimulated by the sense of smell.

Since the beginning of time, spiritual and religious leaders have recognized the olfactory system as a powerful means to induce strong meditative states. Burning frankincense, sandalwood, myrrh, and mugwort began in the ancient temples and until recently was burned in many Catholic churches before services to sanctify the church and induce a holy state amongst the parishioners.

German researchers have discovered that the resin of frankincense, when burned, will actually release a psychoactive substance that elevates the human Spirit to other dimensions of awareness.

Suffice it to say, essential oils affect us in every level of our being. As the soul of the plant, flower, herb and tree, essential oils are the most concentrated form of herbal energy there is. Their applications will vary as much as the direction of form they dictate within a plant, but we are seeing the ability of essential oils to move us beyond the most severe limitations, and touch us in the deepest part of our souls.

The ability of essential oils to address each aspect of our being: the physical, mental, emotional, and spiritual, has been proven throughout the history of their aromatic use.

What is understood by essence, in the pure sense
as used by the medieval alchemists for example,
is the actual energy, the 'soul' of the plant.

Marguerite Maury

Chapter 3

The House of Essence

Temple of Sensuality

... the outer room, balmy with rich perfumes,

should contain a bed, soft, agreeable to the sight,

covered with a clean white cloth,

low in the middle part,

having garlands and bunches of flowers upon it,

and a canopy above it...

There should be a sort of couch besides at the head of this,

a sort of stool on which should be placed

the fragrant ointments for the night...

The Kama Sutra

If we want to gain more understanding into the ceremony of anointing, we should look to the Egyptians for their remarkable use of essential oils. The ceremonies performed in the temples of Egypt were an elaborate mixture of different healing modalities and seemed to always incorporate the five senses. Sight, sound, smell, touch, and taste were all addressed with the anointing ceremonies. Sight was awakened with the anointing, not only was just the intuition and inner vision stimulated, but color rays were often invoked and poured into the body and colored gemstones and crystals were laid upon the body to intone a color vibration into the body.

Music is the harmonious voice of creation;
an echo of the invisible world, one note of the divine
which the entire universe is destined to one day sound.

Mazzini

Chanting and toning were often used to stimulate the auditory system, and were able to shift and clear energy, with the Egyptians being very adept in their knowledge of sound. There are many schools of thought that theorize the Egyptians even used sound vibration to build the ancient pyramids.

Today we have another tool that we can use to stimulate the body, mind, and spirit with sound. A tuning fork is an acoustic resonator in the form of a two pronged fork, with the tines formed from a U-shaped bar usually forged of steel. Tuning forks produce pure musical intervals based on precise mathematical proportions known as the Pythagorean tunings. When we listen to these intervals, there is a resonance created resulting in a physical and psychic re-patterning of our mind, bodies and spirits. The tuning forks have a direct affect on the central nervous system as well, and will greatly help to relax the one receiving the vibrations.

Music. . . a kind of inarticulate, unfathomable speech,
which leads us to the edge of the infinite.

Thomas Carlyle

When using tuning forks, or toning, in combination with essential oils, the ability to shift states of physical, mental, emotional, and spiritual bodies is greatly enhanced.

Another method of inducing sound into the body is through

the art of toning or chanting. When we sing certain sounds (e.g. the sound of OM), we can create a sonic resonance with the sound, and use it to move through the body to affect subtle, vibrational changes, which will enhance the power and frequency of the oils. Essential oils soothe, stimulate and caress the physical with their different frequencies and sensations upon application. The oils can also stimulate, balance, and activate the emotional body, the mental body and the spiritual body. The combination of sound, smell, and touch all combine to create a powerful synergy of change, alignment, balance, integration, purification, and activation, bringing us to the highest level of health in the body, mind and spirit.

The following information chronicles a journey into the House of Essence, the temple of sensuality, or our root chakra. We will journey through the different aspects of each ingredient, which will help to make the House operate at its utmost efficient and radiant optimum.

Take off your shoes and enter into the Home of the Divine.

The House of Essence

We gain entrance to the House of Essence at the base of the spine, the coccyx, sacrum and the perineum. It is here in this temple of sensuality that we find the 1st chakra, or energy center, home to the kundalini, and the place where desire is born. In yogic traditions this house has been referred to as the muladhara, or the fire chakra.

The House of Essence is also the home of ego, and the place where physical survival needs are dictated. We call it the House of Essence, because it is the home of our egoic self, or the physical self, and is oftentimes thought of as our essential self and is the place where we first begin to recognize who we are in the world.

The first House, the House of Essence is the energy center at the root or seat of the spine and is the place where our physical needs originate. The egoic nature sits within this House and is responsible for our survival instincts, like when to come in out of the cold, or when to feed our bodies, or when to quench our thirst. When our ego begins to manifest in our intellectual centers, or the mind we start to encounter difficulty with arrogance and other ego driven emotions, and we might need work to keep the ego from over running our heart based spiritual center.

Our ability to connect into the energy of the earth initiates here, as well as our ability to stay grounded with lofty ideas and belief systems. The first House empowers our connection to physical life. This is also the place where birth occurs within the body, and where we first connect into the physical world at birth, the place where we begin to recognize what it takes to become part of a tribe, or how to survive here on this planet.

This House is awash in deep, rich ruby reds that bring warmth and inspire passion. The bold, grounding color of black is also used to define, ground and balance the physical, mental, emotional and spiritual aspects of this House. The color of red is used to fire up, stimulate and induce passionate, creative forces in the House of Essence. The color black can also be used here to help ground and clear negative energies or forces in the body.

When working with the various Houses during anointing, color is a very valuable assist. There are many ways to embrace and enhance the essence of color. The use of color lamps will invoke the infusion of color, as will the "laying on" of colored gemstones and crystals. ("Laying on" of stones is the actual application of the stone to the body.)

Another very powerful method of working with color is to invoke color rays. When invoking, or petitioning support from the various color rays, it is most beneficial to visualize a brilliant tube or pillar of liquid colored light pouring down from the heavens into the desired House. Allow the vivid hues to fill the House with color, until the light begins to overflow and spill into every cell, while invoking each color ray. The following is an example of an invocation, and in this instance we are invoking the ruby red ray:

Invocation to the Ruby Red Ray

I call upon the Elohim of the Ruby Red Ray, to pour your rich, life sustaining color through this House of Essence. May your passionate red ray strengthen, heal and revitalize every cell of this body. Rich, ruby red ray, spill forth through all of this being, align, balance and spiral into Source.

This invocation is written only to serve as an example and may be amended with any wording that feels more appropriate or more powerful. It's not so much the words used to invoke color, but the intention of inviting color to become a part of the balancing and harmonizing of the House of Essence.

Strength and vitality emanate from this House, and it is here that we connect to our earthly desires, and the physical power of our bodies.

Sound Therapy

It has been written in many ancient texts, that sound was the beginning of creation.

In the first few verses of Genesis we read, ***"And God said, Let there be light, and there was light."*** Quite literally God *said*, denoting that before the light, there was the sound that initiated the creation. In other words, the light of Divine creation was initiated by sound.

More recent texts echo this idea as well. The mystic Sufi master Hazrat Inayat Khan has written, ***"Divine sound is the cause of all manifestation."*** The Greek mathematician Pythagoras noted, ***"The seven heavens sounded each one vowel down to earth and became the creation of all things that be on earth."***

The power of sound has been used since the beginning of time to affect creation, health and well being, and to assist us in moving into deeply meditative states of consciousness and awareness.

Music moves us, and we know not why;
we feel the tears, but cannot trace the source.
***Is it the language of some other state*, born of its memory?**
For what can wake the soul's strong instinct of
another world like music?

L.E. Landon

When singing in this House, or to this House, our temple of sensuality, the tones that resonate the highest here, are most often the sound of a deep MMM or HUM. Toning with the mouth closed allows for the MMM to resonate throughout the body, but can also be consciously directed to the House of Essence, where it will stimulate that chakra.

There is also a corresponding bija, or seed, mantra associated with this chakra. A mantra is a mystic syllable or poem originating in the Vedic religion of India, later becoming an essential part of

Hindu cultures, Buddhist, Sikhism and Jainism traditions. Mantras are now widely used throughout many spiritual traditions based on these earlier Eastern religions. Mantras are thought to carry a sound vibration and can affect the body, mind and Spirit with the appropriate pronunciation of the words. Their intention is to deliver the mind from excessive thought and allow the individual to slip into the Divine Presence of Love. Chanting a mantra is a powerful way to take one deep into the heart of awareness.

That bija mantra is Lam chanted in a one beat rhythm in the pitch of C. While certainly never being limited to these tones and notes, they seem to fire the hearth of this House most effectively. Of course, whenever we sing or tone into the body, our intention should always be to resonate deep into the desired House. Once we have found the note in our toning, we can then direct the sound coming from our mouth directly into the part of the body we choose. When using tuning forks, the notes of C and D have often been found to stimulate this House as well as bring grounding to the physical body.

When using tuning forks to channel sound into the body, we delicately tap the two tuning forks together on the sharp edge of each, and then point the tuning forks towards the body, holding them about 3-4 inches above the body. We can also hold the tuning forks about 8 inches from the ears and circle them so that the sound is not too intense for the ears, but resonates with the auditory channels of the body. The other way to activate tuning forks is to gently rap the end of the tuning fork on the top part of the knee, the fleshy part above the kneecap or the patella. The vibration created is soft, but very palpable to the ears, and can then be used as per instructions above.

It is here in the House of Essence where you will find many glands and organs, the kidneys, adrenal glands, the sexual organs, the bladder, the spine, blood, and the central nervous system. When addressing any physical issues involving any of these organs or glands, it is the House of Essence where you would want to concentrate your energy or work.

The element that calls the House of Essence home is the Earth, blessed Mother Earth, or Gaia, which relates to our grounded earth energy found in the first chakra. The House of Essence is often referred to as the base chakra, and the connection with the Earth is often the most basic connection to being in the physical. So when seeking to ground the body, it is here that we would find our basic, Earthy tendencies. Often we can use the Earth to help ground our bodies and bring them back into physical awareness and balance. Helping to ground the physical body, or bringing awareness to the physicality of the body, can be as simple as walking barefoot on the lawn, taking a barefoot walk along the beach, or just standing barefoot on the Earth and feeling the energies of the Earth, and then let that energy bring us back into our bodies fully, and into the present moment.

Oftentimes when we focus our attention on mental activities, or spend a great deal of time in spiritual pursuits, or have had some emotional shock, we lose touch with our physical nature. Looking to ground the body can help to bring balance back to the physical, mental, emotional and spiritual parts of our selves and enable a more harmonized Earthly existence.

When honoring the directions on the medicine wheel, as is part of the Native American wisdom, we find this House corresponding to the direction of below. When we honor this direction we are in direct Communion with the deep core of the Mother, Earth. When we are fully connected to this direction and the House of Essence, we are in direct relation with the Earth and all her elements and this enables us to develop more Earth-centered spirituality, as well as assisting us to stay grounded in our walk upon the Earth.

Native American traditions believe that all of the directions on the medicine wheel must be in balance in order for all to be right in the world. The four directions of east, south, west and north relate to specific elements as well. East represents the element of air, the south represents fire, the west represents water, and the north represents the Earth. Most teachings follow the path of the four directions, with Mother Earth and Grandfather Sky becoming the directions of below and above, and the body symbolizing the seventh direction, as the conductor between Grandfather Sky and Mother Earth.

Traditionally, we honor the east, west, north and south, with the addition of the below and above helping to integrate the teachings from the four directions.

By staying fully grounded on the Earth, we are able to play in the spiritual realms of Grandfather Sky; in other words, we can soar close to the sun while still being able to walk fully upon the Earth. This corresponds to the more Christian terminology of merging Heaven and Earth. We can become the conduit for that merger of Heaven here on Earth, and that happens through the body. And in order to keep the four directions in balance, the Houses within our body correlating with the four directions must be in balance.

Our ability to connect into the energy of the Earth initiates here in the House of Essence, as well as our ability to stay grounded with lofty ideas and belief systems. The first House empowers our connection to physical life.

When balance reigns within this chakra, the House of Essence, we will feel energetic, centered and grounded in our bodies, empowered, filled with vitality, and with an innate ability to manifest abundance. Those that have achieved balance in this House can also expect that creativity and passion are stimulated and fulfilled. A balanced House assures us that all life can be lived with patience and the knowledge that all is moving according to a Divine plan.

A House that stands divided, or is unbalanced, will influence behavior within us that is often willful, with a distinct lack of self-esteem, manifesting with an inability to achieve goals and a tendency toward self-destructive habits, i.e., addiction is often born in the House of Essence when it is unbalanced.

An imbalance here can often create an atmosphere of fear... fear of abandonment, fear of failure, fear of success, and can often manifest in a lowered sex drive. When imbalance continues to live within this House, we will often become very ego dominant, and can display very destructive manners, becoming overly concerned with personal gratification resulting in very arrogant behaviors. The symptoms of an imbalance in this House manifest first in behavior, and if left unattended for any length of time, will begin to influence the health and well being of the organs and glands associated with this House. It is always much easier to heal imbalance when it manifests in the emotional body, before it manifests into the physical body and begins to produce symptoms of illness.

Diet can often have a very beneficial affect when looking to bring about balance of any of the Houses within the body. Foods prepared and served in the House of Essence to bring harmony and balance to those who indulge in the feast should be rich in red color, tomatoes, beets, red peppers, radishes, plums, cherries, and strawberries. All of these foods will help bring balance, passion, strength, and empowerment to this first House.

Crystals and Gemstones

In the magical realm of crystals and gemstones, we find a plethora of possibilities.

By the Earth that is Her flesh
By the air that is Her breath
By the fire that is Her birthright
By the living waters of Her womb,
And by the stones that are Her bones,
May the Peace of the Goddess
Be with you always.

Priestess Chant

It is the alchemical process of the four elements air, earth, fire and water, combining that produces the magical crystals and gemstones found in the Earth. The power and the magic of the Earth Goddess Gaia, resonates through each and every stone. The House of Essence has built her foundation with gemstones of Ruby, Smoky Quartz, and Obsidian.

The ruby, treasured by the Egyptians, Greeks, and Atlanteans, (as were all crystals and gemstones), carries the fire of creation and passion. Ruby's rich red ray washes over this House, inspiring a sensual vibration of love, the source of all creation. The fire matrix, or kundalini, stimulates this House, and is fed by the ruby. Ruby contains the red fire energy, one of the best stimulants for the kundalini.

The kundalini is an energetic force that is often felt as an orgasmic rush of life that originates in the House of Essence and when properly inspired, can then travel up the spine, awakening all of the Houses in its journey to reach the enlightened center of the crown. This 7th House or crown chakra is often referred to in Eastern literature as the "thousand-petaled lotus". The kundalini is often called the sleeping serpent and is depicted as a coiled snake that sits at the base of the spine.

Yoga practices, pranayama, and meditation techniques will often seek to awaken the kundalini, and coax it to fire up through the spine, awakening the other Houses in its ascension into the crown chakra, or House of Wisdom, bringing us into heightened states of awareness and deep states of meditation and bliss.

The gemstone ruby also inspires energy and high hope, helping us to build life force, and assists with the enhancement of our love of self. However, the ruby can often stimulate the emotion of anger, and if used on someone who is irritable or angry, there might be some intensive transmutation that will need to occur to harmonize the anger. The ruby works with the rich red ray of illumination, and when we lay the ruby upon the body and then visualize a ruby ray pulsing through the stone and into the body, all aspects will be intensified. This would be a good time to invoke the Ruby Red Ray.

Ruby is an excellent stone for using as protection when out in the world to ward off negative energies and can be used to clear out negative energies in the body as well. Ruby is also a stone that can be used to stimulate sexual activity and enhance desire.

When working with gemstones and crystals, it is important to clear, and then charge the crystals before we use them. Whenever we acquire a gemstone, it is recommended that the crystal be bathed in a sea-salt water bath for 24 hours and then, bathed in the moonlight and a few hours of sunlight to thoroughly cleanse and clear the crystals. Once that is complete, take the crystals between the hands and charge them with good intentions, whether it be healing thoughts, balancing, or activating energy. Focus positive energy into the crystal and it can even be placed upon our altars to be charged up amongst the sacred objects, and it will then be ready to be placed upon the body.

Smoky quartz is a sacred stone that heralds back to the time of the ancient Druids. The deep smoky, grey, or brown-black crystal assists with the magnetic attraction of abundance. It works well with the House of Essence due to the fact that it is here in this House that the fire of our physical creations is sparked. The deep Earthy color of smoky quartz helps to ground us with its deep, smoky visions of Earth, and is brilliant in its ability to help connect life force into our physical beings. Smoky quartz is a wonderful stone to help in dispelling depression as its grounding influence helps to bring us more into present time with a sense of pride about being in physical form. Smoky quartz helps with the integration of Spirit into form.

Smoky quartz carries a very high vibration and as such, helps to purify negativity and auric debris. However, one of its greatest offerings is the ability to draw the love force of the heart down into the House of Essence, enhancing the fires of creation.

Smoky quartz is also a stone to use when looking to enhance the acceptance of the physical body as it helps clear fear and negativity from the House of Essence and allows for a clear flow of passionate kundalini energy.

It is important when using smoky quartz, or any other stone to help draw out negative energies from the body, that once we have finished working with the stone, we then purify the crystal in a salt-water bath. After bathing the crystals, we would then need to charge the stone again before using on the body.

Obsidian, the third stone of our foundation in the House of Essence, is another power player. Obsidian is a deep, dark black stone that was created from molten lava that cooled and crystal-lized. Obsidian is another very grounding stone, and helps with the integration of the more etheric Houses (the upper chakras) into the more physical Houses (the lower chakras). (Lower and higher, only in the third dimensional visual scope of relating not in the actual value of the Houses.)

Obsidian helps us to purify and refine our higher ideals of ego. Obsidian has often been called the "Warrior of Truth" and helps to dissipate anger in this House, particularly well when combined with the essential oil of patchouli. This "Warrior of Truth," obsidian, will also help to awaken any dormant potential hidden within us waiting to be inspired. Obsidian also carries the deep grounding effects of its distant relative, smoky quartz. Obsidian carries very cathartic qualities and is excellent at bringing the truth to the surface very quickly, which can help to release emotional and energetic blocks. Quite often obsidian will bring to the surface the shadow qualities of our personality for discernment and healing.

Obsidian's sibling, snowflake obsidian, helps us when balancing the light and dark aspects of our selves, and helps to break negative conditioned patterns. Snowflake obsidian puts out the welcome mat to higher forces seeking to assist this House with creative manifestation.

Essential Oils

*In a world sayable and lush, where marvels
offer themselves up readily for verbal dissection,
smells are often right on the tip of our tongues -but no
closer- and it gives them a kind of magical distance,
a mystery, a power without a name, a sacredness."*

Diane Ackerman

With a wafting of heavenly fragrance, we enter the alchemical, aromatic world of essential oils.

The first player for the House of Essence is vetiver, Vetiveria zizanioides; originating in tropical and semitropical climates, this grass is a close relative of lemongrass. The roots of the plants contain the most amount of essential oil and they are what are used to produce the best vetiver. For optimum distillation, the roots should be at least two years old before distilling to produce the dark brown oil with its warm, spicy, Earthy and woody smell.

The oil from Reunion is considered the best in the world, requiring 1 ton of plant to produce just 7 pounds of essential oil.

Vetiver is a very effective oil to inhale when visualizing abundance. It seeks to assist when manifesting money. Vetiver's rich, Earthy, musty fragrance is very grounding, helping us to connect deeply with the Earth.

Vetiver has antiseptic properties and is quite relaxing, helping those with insomnia. Vetiver is also an excellent oil to be used for auric protection. While inhaling the enticing, woody aroma of vetiver, we would want to visualize a protective field of energy encapsulating our body. The halo of vetiver will wrap us up in its protective grace. Vetiver is a very powerful ally when looking to feel completely comfortable with our physicality and our connection to the Earth.

Ylang ylang, Canaga odorata, another native of the island of Reunion, is also grown in Madagascar and the Philippines. Ylang ylang is a large, softly weeping tree, with fragrant, intoxicating yellow flowers that are picked when mature, to produce the essential oil. At the age of ten, the tree is capable of producing as much as 33 pounds of oil.

Research has shown Ylang ylang to be of great assist in reducing fevers with its antiseptic properties. The heady, sensual fragrance of ylang ylang is a powerful aphrodisiac, and when inhaled or used in proper formulation, can shift impotence and frigidity.

The oil of ylang ylang, a mistress in the House of Essence, has a powerful, heady, hypnotic, sweet floral aroma, reminiscent of the narcissus or hyacinth.

Ylang ylang is of great importance when seeking to calm tension and stress, to lift negativity, and to increase sensuality in the House of Essence. Ylang ylang is also a great stimulator for the kundalini, the fire of life.

Ylang ylang is a magnet for attracting the essence of love and sensuality into the 1st House, the House of Essence, and the temple of our sensuality.

Patchouli, Pogostemon cablin, waltzes into the House of Essence, distilled from the leaves and young shoots of an herbaceous shrub that grows to a height of about 3 feet. Patchouli is a native of Malaysia, but is now cultivated in many other parts of the world as well.

The oil of patchouli is imbued with a deep, woody, Earthy, and spicy smell, and elicits a heady, sensual energy.

Patchouli is a wonderful oil to use in skin care preparations due to its anti-inflammatory and antiseptic properties.

The fragrance of patchouli, with its musky sweetness, is very useful when looking to arouse sexual desire, and has long been used for such aphrodisiac properties. Patchouli is also very useful when desiring to manifest and attract money into one's life. It stimulates the House of Essence into its creative ability to manifest abundance. It can be blended with ginger and frankincense to create an abundance blend, which can then be used in mediation and anointing to help with the manifestation of abundance on all levels.

Patchouli, with its roots dug deeply into the Earth, helps us to become more firmly rooted to the Earth, assisting the fulfillment of physical and survival needs.

Patchouli is a great essential oil to use when looking to clear anger from the House of Essence. Patchouli a friend indeed, resonates highest with its air of sensuality, in the House of Essence.

(Remember, when using these recommended essential oils, stones, colors, sounds, foods, etc., these are guidelines based on years of practice, experience and wisdom. However, we are never limited in our intuitive wisdom by these standards, and I would only hope to set a frame of reference where we can grow and change as our own intuition dictates.) Working with all of these tools is a powerful way to develop our intuition fully, and from there ... we become completely unlimited in our choices.

Anointing the House of Essence

Whenever we seek to perform an anointing ceremony it is best for the ceremony to be performed in front of an altar, or in a sacred space created for meditation or ceremony. An altar is created to establish an aura of reverence and a place for the sacred to occur. An altar is an elevated place, platform, dais or structure that has been constructed and used traditionally as the site of a religious or spiritual ceremony, prayer, and or, meditation. It is often covered with prayer cloths or some other sacred piece of fabric, and has offerings laid upon it of spiritual significance in honor of the Divine. When creating an altar always ask for the presence of the Divine, and invoke a blessing of consecration upon the altar. The altar can be as simple or as ornate as one desires, but should without exception, include holy or spiritual objects, and can also have offerings of fresh flowers, candles, pictures of religious or spiritual masters, teachers, or guides, food, as well as crystals, gemstones, feathers, or any other personal item that is significant. The altar should be created in a place that will continue to be used for meditation, prayer and ceremony, as the energy created there can be used again and again to connect back into the Divine through a daily practice or devotion that could include prayer and meditation, mantra work, chanting, yoga, etc.

When preparing the anointing chrism, or oil, light the candles on the altar, place fresh flowers or fresh fruit as an offering to the Divine. It is best to create an anointing chrism on either the new moon, or full moon as the energies of the moon are very powerful and can imbue the chrism with additional strength. After the oils have been created, we can then put the oil in the light of the full moon to charge it even further.

We will want to have a clean, sterilized bottle for the chrism with either a dropper top, or an orifice reducer top with lid. These can be found online or from distributors of essential oils.

When we create a chrism specifically for the House of Essence, prepare the anointing blend using the prescribed essential oils of ylang ylang, patchouli and vetiver, and use a total of 28 drops of essential oils to one ounce of carrier oil such as organic jojoba, or for short term use, organic olive oil. The majority of the blend should be patchouli, so we would first pour a desired amount of patchouli, followed by vetiver, and then lastly, the ylang ylang as it is overwhelmingly strong in its aroma, remembering to use a total of 28 drops of essential oils per one-ounce bottle of carrier oil. It is a good idea to put the essential oils in first, and then fill the remainder of the bottle with the chosen carrier oil. Be sure to use at least a one-ounce bottle for the anointing chrism. Once the oils have all been added to the bottle, add the carrier oil to fill the bottle, cap it and take it between the palms and rub the palms back and forth, allowing the oils to emulsify together.

We will then want to take the chrism and invoke the presence of the Divine, Christ, Angelic hosts, Great Spirit, or God, to come and consecrate the anointing blend. Ask for the Divine Christ light to come and consecrate the anointing oil so that it shall be holy and able to differ that holiness upon the body.

It would be a good idea to then allow the oil to be infused with moonlight, and then placed upon the altar where it can gather even more power. We would want to bring the oil inside before sunrise, as we would not want the oils to be exposed to sunlight, which can affect the potency of the oils.

When it is time to perform the ceremony to balance the House of Essence, again, light the candles on the altar, sit in mediation or prayer and ask for the presence of the Divine, beckon all angelic masters and guides who guide, aid and assist us to be present and to offer any assistance in the ceremony. In that deep and reverent state, take the anointing oil and pour a few drops into the palm of the hand, and rub on the tailbone, pubic bone, perineum, or the sides of the hips, and soles of the feet. Hold the hand over the oils directly on the skin where the oils have been rubbed, to help the oils penetrate into the body. While we have our hand on the body, it is advisable to focus sending healing energy through the hand, the oils and into the body. We want to hold our hand on the body for at least five minutes to allow the oils to penetrate the skin and be absorbed by the tissues and bloodstream. As essential oils are very volatile, they evaporate quickly and by holding the hand on the body we assure that they penetrate rather than evaporate.

We can then choose a crystal from the above-mentioned crystals, and lay the crystal directly on the skin, on top of the oils. All the while invoke healing energy, color, and light into the area, and begin to tone or sing into the crystal or use your tuning forks to invoke sound into the body. We could also invoke the color ray that corresponds to this House, which would be a rich, ruby red.

We would then use our tuning forks (C and D) and gently tap them on the patella of the knee, then circle the tuning forks 6-8 inches away from the ears so that the sound can enter the body and activate the House of Essence. We could also aim the end of the tuning forks at the House of Essence as close to the body without touching it, so that the sound carries deeply into the 1st House. If we don't have tuning forks to use, or with us, we can begin to intone the bija mantra of Lam, or chant the tone MMM, and let it resonate throughout this chakra

Lying in front of the altar assures that the ceremony is taking place in a sanctified area, and the oils are assisted in helping to bring the House back into alignment, balance, integration and activation.

If we want we can anoint one House at a time, or we can create elaborate anointing ceremonies where we anoint all of the Houses in the body with each corresponding anointing chrism. We would begin with the House of Essence and its specific anointing chrism and work our way up to each subsequent House and its specific anointing chrism, until we come the House of Spirit, or the 7th chakra.

We can anoint ourselves, or our loved ones. We can anoint ourselves on a daily basis with the anointing blends designed to help balance each House or we can create ceremonies that happen only once in our life, such as the Baptismal ceremony or sacrament, or any of the other ceremonies described throughout this book.

It is important to recognize that when we perform an anointing ceremony on one of our loved ones, or ourselves, and include the different modalities described, the affects can be very powerful, and often quite life changing. We would always want to hold the space for that to occur, and fully support ourselves, and our loved ones in making that shift into physical, emotional, mental, and or spiritual awareness. Begin the anointing always by asking that the angels of anointing assist in bringing an aura of protection around all involved in the ceremony, and ask that all work be done for the highest possible good of the one being anointed, and also ask for balance, harmony and alignment to occur within all of the Houses, the emotional, mental and spiritual bodies.

Anointing with sanctified essential oils can have very profound effects and can often manifest physically in the form of nausea, dizziness, stimulated dreams, emotional release, and sometimes even physical release. The effects of anointing can last for quite some time after the experience, as the oils will actually penetrate the skin and enter the bloodstream, affecting us metabolically, the effects lasting for days and sometimes weeks.

Anointing is a very powerful tool from an ancient time and place that is being resurrected again to assist us in a modern era, to help us move into higher states of consciousness and to promote health and well being in the physical, mental, emotional, and spiritual bodies.

Chapter 4

The House of Water

Temple of Emotions

Aphrodite went away to Cyprus,

and entered her fragrant temple at Paphos,

where she had a precinct and a fragrant altar.

After going inside,

she closed the bright doors

and the Graces gave her a bath

they oiled her with sacred olive oil,

the kind that the Gods always have on,

that pleasant ambrosia that she was perfumed with.

The Homeric Hymns

Welcome to the House of Water, the abode of vital force, and the seat of our emotional creativity. The House of Water is home to our emotional being, and is therefore the seat of our feelings and beliefs. As well as the emotions, the House of Water is home to desire and lives within the realm of the 2nd chakra. It is referred to as the swadisthana in yogic traditions, and is also the home of our intuitive knowledge, the place where we feel our gut instincts.

This House of Water is one of the most important energy centers; because it is here that our relationship to self, as well as our relations with others becomes established. In this House, the merger of duality, between the polarized aspects of our selves, and true merger with the Divine is begun. Sexual union is stimulated here in this Earthy colored home, and the desire to come into relationship with members of our tribe, community, or village is initiated here also. When we are first born, it is here in the House of Water that we first begin to establish our relationship with the world around us. We acknowledge our physicality in the 1st House, and from there, in the 2nd House we begin to establish our relationships to others.

As we begin to spend time here we find that our ability to relate to others is in direct alignment with our ability to connect to the deepest part of our selves. When healing and balance occur here, there is no impediment to the merger with the yin and yang aspects of our being. It is then possible to begin the process of falling in love with our selves, and the subsequent establishment of loving relationships with others. When we come into a balanced state within the House of Water, or the 2nd chakra, we begin to heal areas of separation from Source, or God, within ourselves, which then begins to manifest outwardly in our relationship to others.

As we move more into balance in the outside world, we are more aware of the principles of manifestation, or the ability to make our dreams a reality. This House is the place where manifestation of abundance on all levels is fulfilled. Working in tandem with the 1st House, where desire to manifest is initiated; we can then use the creative emotional juice within the 2nd House to bring the manifestation into reality. The key ingredient to the manifestation of abundance and our overall receptivity to it, is generosity of spirit, or how we share our selves with the world. It is a universal law that we give as we receive. Gold finds its way into the heart of a man who gives more, and is of better service, as surely as the sun rises in the east. When we give, we are also creating more space to receive; it is an even flow of energy that gets exchanged. As we heal any areas within ourselves that still hold others at a distance, we can then enlist our relationships and the network that they provide to add fuel to the fire of manifestation.

As we begin to explore our inner self, through all methods of self-inquiry, we start to recognize where we might be holding onto any level of separation from Spirit, or God. When we begin to recognize that the only path to true, unbridled happiness lies within us, and the recognition of our own Divinity, we can begin to cultivate practices that allow us to move more and more into a state of union within ourselves, with our own state of God consciousness. The more we move into that state, the more we are able to manifest our dreams, as it is God, or the Divine state within, that is the sole source of our supply.

As we come to recognize ourselves as God, we also begin to embody the traits of a creator God, which allows us to create our own reality, and that is the key to manifesting our dreams of abundance. It is within this chakra, the House of Water that this relationship occurs. As we begin to manifest, it is in the sharing with others that our true wealth begins to build. All relationships initiate in the House of Water, it is the abode of our emotions. The act of sharing our abundance with others, when we give in proportion to what we receive, the flow of give and take are in equal balance, always allowing for Source to flow into us, unimpeded, as it flows out of us, thus reducing any constriction in the flow.

The House of Water aligns with the direction of the south on the medicine wheel in Native American wisdom. This direction is associated with the season of summer, a time of abundance and fruitfulness, and is generally a time of great growth.

This House lives in the neighborhood 1-2 inches below the navel, and feeds the first lumbar region, as well as the sacrum, the pelvis, the sexual organs of women, and the hips. Whenever there is an imbalance in this House, those areas can eventually begin to manifest the symptoms of the imbalance i.e. low back issues, sexual dysfunctions, hip problems etc.

This House feeds creativity, as the fire of the Kundalini moves in to drive the desire to create. Whenever we are lacking creativity in our lives, we would most certainly be experiencing some level of deficiency or imbalance in the House of Water.

The foods laid upon the banquet table that would best serve those who reside within this temple, are from the orange food group, oranges, carrots, apricots, peaches, pumpkins, persimmons, eggs, calcium and vitamin C. Eating any of the foods within this food group will help to bring balance into this House and align our emotional beings.

The walls of this House are softly washed in the warm, rich hues of carnelian orange. The soft glow of light that filters in to enliven this House, bathes us in healing color. To enhance the resonance of color in this House, we may use the following invocation:

Invocation to the Carnelian Orange Ray

I call upon the Elohim (or the Angels)
of the Carnelian Orange Ray,
to pour vitality of Divine Source
through my second House of Water.
May your healing carnelian color,
bathe my home of desires and emotions.
Evocative, orange carnelian ray,
spill forth through all of my being,
align, balance, and spiral into Source.

Sound Therapy

The lyrical vibrations that most closely resonate in this House are filled with the tones of UMM and UHH (as in drum), and the notes of E. The tuning forks we would use are the C and E forks. The bija mantra used to balance this House is Vam chanted to a two beat rhythm. When chanting or toning a mantra, it is beneficial to visualize the sound vibrating throughout this House.

When this House is balanced, all who come here will find themselves inspired creatively, intuitively, and will also recognize stability within the emotional bodies. There will be a strong relationship with the Divine, supported by a stalwart belief system and spiritual practice. Relationships will be healthy and fulfilling when one has balance in this House. When the House of Water is completely in alignment and balanced, one would find a great deal of optimism with a compassionate sense of belonging. This House, when balanced, will also tend to bring harmony to sexuality and the merger of our dualistic natures, celebrating the marriage of the male and the female parts of our selves. The male aspects provide a place for the feminine to become a womb of creativity, which inevitably leads to a healthy, balanced sexual relationship with our partners as well.

There is a dramatic difference when this House is not balanced. Those who live within the imbalance will find themselves exhibiting addictive and aggressive tendencies, and may appear selfish, manipulative, emotionally explosive, or socially withdrawn.

We would also look to the House of Water to address problems with sexual guilt, and fertility issues, or any other issues around sexuality.

Crystals and Gemstones

The foundation of this House is built with alchemical gemstones, which form a partnership of strength and support. There are many rulers in the kingdom of gemstones that serve to bring their magical properties from the crystalline realm of the Earth into our temples where we may partake of their extraordinary magic.

Jasper is a stone popular since antiquity. Jasper has been considered a magic stone by many, and a Native American name for the stone meant "rainbringer." The House of Water is fed by rain, to fill the emotional pools that surround this temple of emotions.

This stone has been used to assist in warding off negativity by encasing one in an aura of protective, tangerine orange color. Jasper assists with the harmonizing of the House of Water, by balancing desire and creativity, as well as balancing the yin and yang, or the feminine and masculine aspects of our selves.

Jasper is a wonderful stone, which can be laid upon the House of Water, bringing its deep orange color and balancing energy to help align and stimulate this temple of our emotions.

Its partner and a cornerstone of this House, is the Carnelian. Carnelian was a stone worn in Egypt to promote peace and harmony. It has even been said that it was used to assist the mummy, when buried together, with resurrection into the afterlife. Carnelian has also been said to contain within the stone, the magical power and virtue of the Goddess Isis.

The Moslems believed that the carnelian assisted with the creation of all desires. Carnelian has been noted to assist with the balancing of the thyroid gland, and its vibration is closest to the vibration of the sacral chakra, or the House of Water.

Carnelian is a power stone, often called the Gem of the Earth. It carries a Mars like energy, and when worn at night, will help to halt nightmares. Carnelian also boosts our ability to manifest goals, by its stimulation of the adrenal gland. Carnelian is a powerful stone to assist us with restoring vitality and inspires great motivation, which aids in the manifestation of goals and creativity. Carnelian is said to dispel anger and banish emotional negativity.

Essential Oils

In the abundantly aromatic world of essential oils, the first oil to assist with the balancing and activation of the House of Water is orange, or the botanical name, Citrus auranticum sinensis.

The orange tree grows worldwide but we find the best oil production occurs mostly in France, Spain, Italy, California, Florida, Israel, and Brazil. The essential oil of orange is expressed from the skin of the fruit. It is very easy to witness the essential oil of orange as we peel an orange in the sun. When we break into the orange peel, the droplets of essential oil molecules are released, and are visually seen exploding into the air, and is a natural way of diffusing the oil into the air. Soon afterwards, the refreshing citrus scent, wafts up your nose, inspiring the mouth to water. It is the release of essential oils that create that explosion of scent from the peel of the orange, and all other citrus for that matter.

Orange essential oil is excellent for dispelling depression, and inspiring joy and vitality within. (I have not witnessed a face that did not smile when I waved the essence of orange beneath the nose.) The essential oil of orange is a happy note, with child-like joyful enthusiasm, and has a fresh, vital and clean aroma.

The essential oil of orange works with the Mars energy to bring inspiration to our creations, and happiness to our psyches. The frequency of orange oil works very well with the vibration of the House of Water, serving to balance and integrate the sacral chakra and brings a lightness and sweetness to the emotional being.

Orange has a very calming influence on children when inhaled, or on anyone who suffers from being overly tired. As with all citrus oils, the use of them on the skin before exposure to the sun may cause photosensitivity, and caution should be used when using any of the citrus oils for that reason.

Another of the sacred giants in the essential oil kingdom will certainly be spruce, Tsuga canadensis.

The essential oil of spruce, the gentle giant of wisdom, comes from a large evergreen found to be native to the West Coast of North America. Like a walk through a spruce forest just after a rain when the oil droplets are stimulated into a dance of the senses, the essential oil also has a clean, fresh, balsamic sweetness to its scent. The fragrance is strong, green, and woody, bringing strength, courage and conviction to the psyche.

The hypnotic notes of spruce create a relaxing, soothing and peaceful balm to the soul. Within that spell, we sense protection, a feeling of sacred space around us.

Spruce helps us to connect with the Earth, uniting Heaven and Earth within us. The ancient trees, the dolphins, and whales hold a sacred trinity of truth and wisdom. They each wait for our arrival to share this great wisdom, and sacred knowledge. The essential oil of spruce aids in our stand of majesty and our integration of ancient wisdom. The essential oil of spruce can be used whenever we seek to bring courage, strength and vitality to our system or to any endeavor we undertake. Spruce brings courage and valor to the emotional body, along with bringing a sense of rooted grounding and strength to the sacral realm of the body.

Another powerful player in the world of essential oils used to balance the House of Water would be clary sage. The beautiful, strongly aromatic clary sage, Salvia sclarea, grows to a height of about three feet, and delivers its powerful oil from the flowers, leaves and stems.

Clary sage is a well known euphoric and an excellent assist to the female hormonal system, as it contains phyto-hormones. (It is contraindicated in pregnancy, as are many essential oils. In fact, one might want to consider not using oils at all on anyone who is pregnant and has not been previously exposed to essential oils as the oils can transfer directly into the fetus and become even more powerful).

Clary sage can be massaged directly into the reflex points of the feet to reduce the cramping that often comes with a woman's monthly cycle. Those reflex points are on the back of the leg, along either side of the Achilles tendon from the heel up four inches or so. Using about 4 drops of clary sage per foot, massage the oil into the points and allow about 3-4 minutes of massage to be sure that the oils are absorbed. That area might even be a bit sore, corresponding to the cramping of the pelvic region.

Clary sage is one of the most powerful oils we have to help balance the emotions. With the green, herbal aroma of clary sage, we sink into deep, relaxed states of tranquility, and its somewhat sensuous fragrance helps to induce dreaming, (not an oil to inhale before or during driving.)

Clary sage also helps to calm children upon inhalation, and can be a powerful anti-depressant. The musky aroma will warm and relax both the body and mind.

The name clary sage is derived from the Latin word salvere, or "to save," or another name salvia salvatrix, "the plant which saves and heals." It has been written that the Egyptians used clary sage in a remedy against the plague. As is true with most essential oils, clary sage has strong anti-viral and anti-bacterial properties and could very well be used to help ward against the plague. Clary sage can also be used to calm the mind before sleeping, helping to induce a sweet and restful sleep.

Anointing the House of Water

When we recognize the need to bring the House of Water back into balance, we can simply anoint ourselves, and the 2nd chakra with the consecrated anointing oil designed specifically for this House, or we can incorporate all of the Houses into a ceremony that allows each House to be anointed using the specific oils for each blend.

We would also use all of the tuning forks, tones and seed sounds to help align and balance each House in the ceremony. The ceremony can be as elaborate or as simple as one desire's, again; the most important part of any anointing is always the intention set before, during and after the ceremony.

We would most certainly want to perform the anointing in front of our altar, in a sacred space designed to welcome the presence of the Divine.

An altar that is specifically designed to work on balancing the House of Water, would want to include items that represent the emotional body, perhaps some orange fruit, orange candles, a bowl of water or vessel of water would be a good representation of the watery nature of our emotional body. When we place vessels or bowls of water to represent the element of water, recognize that water is also a great conductor of energy, and can absorb energies as well. Often times during an anointing session, we can release emotions or feelings that may no longer serve us, and the water can absorb those toxins and so once the ceremony is completed, we would want to pour the water out in our garden. The Earth is then able to absorb anything released and recreate the energies into powerful positive forces. Also on the altar would be any stones or crystals that would be used in the anointing ceremony. (Again remembering that all crystals should be cleaned and charged before and after using on the body)

We would ideally want to create our anointing blend on a new moon, or full moon, before the ceremony is to occur so that we can then harness the power of the moon and consecrate our chrism with those energies. To create an anointing chrism for the House of Water, we would take an empty bottle and begin to pour the oil of spruce into the bottle, followed by the oil of orange, and lastly, the oil of clary sage. Again, the safety standard is 28 drops of essential oil to one ounce of carrier oil, either organic jojoba, or for short-term use only, organic olive oil. Once the bottle is capped, we would take the bottle between our palms and rub the bottle back and forth, allowing the oils to mix completely within the carrier oil. At this time we will also be wanting to invoke the presence and the power of the Divine, a simple invocation calling for the presence and the holiness of Heavenly realms, the angelic hosts and all power of God to infuse the anointing chrism, so that the anointing oils become blessed, sanctified, and consecrated.

We could then place the oils in the light of the moon to gather the forces of the moonlight, and afterwards place the oil on the altar until the time of the ceremony.

When the anointing ceremony occurs, and it is time to anoint the House of Water, we would take the blessed chrism and pour a few drops into the palm of our hand and then rub the oils onto the lower belly of the 2nd chakra, and we could also anoint the sacral area of the spine.

As mentioned before, we would want to hold our hand over the oils on the skin for about 3-5 minutes to allow for the oils to penetrate the skin and enter the bloodstream. The very intention we invoked into the oils should be in our thoughts as we allow our intention for the one being anointed to be consecrated, aligned, and balanced in the physical, mental, emotional and spiritual bodies. Again, remember that the emotional body sits within the House of Water, and as such, tremendous emotional release can occur when anointing this particular House. It is important for the one administering the anointing to be able to hold that person as any release wants to happen, until the energy of release, be it through tears, laughter or kriyas (physical buckling or shaking of the body generated through intense energy moving through the body) in the body subsides, at which time it would be appropriate to take the hand away and continue.

After the appropriate amount of time holding the area of the 2nd House, we could then take one of the crystals set upon the altar, carnelian or jasper and lay the stone upon the House of Water, invoking the orange color to be infused into the body.

We could then use our tuning forks and allow the sounds to permeate that area of the body. By striking the tuning forks of C and E on the soft part of the patella, or striking them lightly against each other, we can direct the ends of the tuning forks into the House of Water or wave the tuning forks above the body in that general area. We would want to hold the resonating tuning forks 6 inches away from the ears and allow the sound to vibrate into the head as this combination of C and E also stimulates the intuitive vision of the 6th House as well. We could also tone the bija mantra of Vam, or tone the sound of UMM, or UHH into the body as well.

Recognize that anointing this House can cause a great deal of discomfort, or for some even nausea as old emotional blocks are released. Hold the area, perhaps putting another hand over the heart, and allow the release to occur, and do not move away from the House until the body and emotion become still again. Sit with the anointing and allow for the full expression of the work to be done before moving on to the next House, or sitting quietly in meditation.

If anointing all of the Houses, we would then transition to the next House, and continue to work our way up the body. If we are only anointing this part of the body, we would then give thanks for the blessing and allow the energy of the anointing its due course.

Please remember, these are all just guidelines and can be amended as our intuition guides us, it will always be the intention put into the ceremony that creates its true power.

Also know that after the anointing has occurred and for some time afterwards, up to a few weeks, molecular changes may occur and induce symptoms that are somewhat unexplainable, such as emotional outbursts, dizziness, nausea, or excessive elimination. This is symptomatic of the anointing continuing to affect the physical molecular body as well as the mind and spirit in its healing. The oils have the ability to absorb into the epidermis of the skin, then seep into the dermis layer of the skin where the oils then penetrate into the cellular system of our bodies, and will continue to change us, heal us, and allow us to come fully into alignment within the physical, mental and emotional bodies. One of the true gifts of anointing is that we will continue to feel the effects long after the initial anointing occurs. By anointing ourselves on a daily basis we are continually asking to be immersed into the evolutionary path of self realization, or the recognition of ourselves as Divine, and anything that stands in the way of that will be released from the body, and hence allow healing to come to the physical aspect of our selves.

There are also a few ways in which we can aid the release of any emotions that are triggered from the anointing. Laughing, crying, somatic breath work, vocalizing (singing or yelling, hopefully in the car with all the windows rolled up) or through the processes of elimination.

Anointing can inspire all of these to occur, and if the trauma, or wounding that needs to be healed is deep, it may take more than one anointing to affect a dramatic change within the body, but IT WILL OCCUR with continued use of the anointing chrism.

Chapter 5

The House of Transcendence

Temple of Transmutation

I feel that all the stars shine in me,

The world breaks into my life like a flood,

The flowers blossom in my body.

All the youthfulness of land and waters smoke

Like an incense in my heart;

And the breath plays on my thoughts as on a flute.

Rabindranath Tagore

Welcome home to the House of Transcendence, our temple of transmutation. This House is located in the area above the navel and below the diaphragm. It is most often referred to as the solar plexus, and is the very central core of our being, and the place where we focus on our personal power. In yogic terms, this area is referred to as the manipura and is the 3rd chakra in the body. This House is located adjacent to the two lower Houses, and form a trinity referred to as the kanda, or the bulb, and constitute the region of fire in ayurvedic traditions.

In this House, the transmutation of greed, guilt and all those fear-based emotions are received and assessed from the 2nd House, and can then be synthesized and melted into love with the power of the solar plexus and the love from the heart of the 4th House. It is here in the 3rd House that the transmutation occurs. Once those fears and negative emotions have been transmuted, we can then begin to build a cone of personal power in this center. When this House is completely balanced, we will feel completely safe in the world, and able to express our truth with certainty and assurance.

This chakra is called the House of Transcendence because we can learn to identify any issues of separation, fear and withholding in the 2nd House, and move those emotions into this House where our seat of power can then use the love from the 4th House, the heart center to burn up the fears in a cauldron of love, and turn that fear into power, generating strength and personal command in the solar plexus.

In Native American wisdom, this energy center serves the direction of the east on the medicine wheel. The east represents springtime, a time of renewal when life bursts forth after the internal exploration and hibernation of winter. The east is the direction of the rising sun, which is a powerful energy that can bring the essence of illumination and fruition to our dreams.

The House of Transcendence is the center of personal power and the place where our passion to serve is also ignited. We must ask our selves in the discovery of personal power and the subsequent desire to serve, (not only our selves, but also others,) to whom and what do we serve, and why? Do we serve our selves to the exclusion of others, indicating a somewhat self-centered or possibly arrogant power, which is generally ego driven, or do we seek to serve in a Divinely inspired way? Do we look to make our actions, our words, and even our thoughts serve the whole, or the greater good, thus affecting a positive change for all of humanity, or do our thoughts, words and actions reflect a desire to please only the self, these are all questions that help to determine whether or not we are in complete alignment and balance in our solar plexus, the seat of our power and the House of Transcendence.

As we started to discover in the House of Water any feelings of separation from Source, or the Divine, or God, and began to heal those wounds, it's here in the House of Transcendence that we truly become empowered as we begin to recognize that the source of our power is actually the Divine part of our selves. We can become very empowered with that wisdom, and in that empowered place, we are capable of manifesting all of our hearts desires. As we become aware of our power to manifest as Divine creators, it is important that we temper wisdom with humility, so as to keep the ego in check. It is here in the House of Transcendence that our personal power can be used to fuel the manifestation of our creativity from the 2nd House. It is also here where we build and maintain our own personal power, and at the opposite side of the spectrum, where we give our power away and deplete our seat of strength.

As we bring harmony and balance into this House, the recognition of our own Divine nature and power can then inspire a realization that everyone around us is also that spark of Divinity expressing itself in human form, and with this empowered knowledge we can begin to look at how we might serve others. As was said earlier, it is in the equal exchange of giving and receiving that we find true abundance and balance in our lives.

This House is a home where we can send the newly established relationships with others, initiated in the 2nd House, to be nurtured and fed with our passion and power. The House of Transcendence is where we find gratitude for all the relationships in our lives, and the place where we can begin to work on the strengthening of those relationships.

This House lives in the center of our bodies, the 3rd chakra or solar plexus, found above the navel and below the breastbone, and the area of the 8th thoracic. In Chinese medicine, we call this House the triple warmer and it is an area of the body to investigate when looking to define our purpose and the wisdom of our work. The true mission of our lives is called dharma in Buddhist traditions, and it's a Sanskrit term meaning, "that which upholds or supports". In its most frequent usage, dharma means, "right way of living, proper conduct". When we are truly balanced in the House of Transcendence, we are in our power, balanced between the physical and spiritual, and capable of living our true dharma. This 3rd House is home to our dharma as it is the place where we interpret our intuitive instincts, those gut reactions initiated in the 2nd House, which guide us to our higher purpose, or our true mission in life.

The foods that most support the House of Transcendence and help bring balance to our power center are foods in the yellow food group, bananas, corn, lemons, melons, butter, pineapples, papaya, yams, starches and all those of like color.

Similarly, the color ray that you would want to work with in this House is the color of golden yellow, topaz, like the golden rays of the sun; these are the shades of color that most warm this House. One could wear clothing of this color range, or colored gemstones to help empower this energy center, or we could invoke and visualize a golden yellow color ray pouring into this area of the body which would also be very beneficial in bringing balance and harmony to this House.

Invocation to the Topaz Yellow Ray

I call upon the Elohim of the Topaz Yellow Ray,
To pour your vital color into, and through
My third House of Transcendence,
Radiant topaz yellow ray
Awaken Divine purpose within me.
Revitalizing yellow topaz ray
Spill forth through all of my being,
Align, balance, and spiral into Source.

When we call upon higher powers to bring color into us, it is as if radiant sunbeams illuminate through and around this House, bringing warmth, direction, and illumination to our lives.

The element of air resides in this temple, empowering us with breath, and it is here that the diaphragm begins the journey of breath. By working with breathing exercises to bring the breath all the way down into the solar plexus or 3rd House, we are empowering this center with oxygen and vitality. This House is also an area we can work with to assist in the emotional healing of our 2nd House, and a very good place to express gratitude and appreciation. By gathering strength from the solar plexus, we can channel that strength into the 2nd House of Water to empower the release of negative emotions and replace them with optimism and enthusiasm.

As the element of air exists in this House, it is the place to initiate singing and chanting. If we can begin the sound here when we sing or chant, we can infuse the sound with a solid, powerful expression of energy.

When illuminating this House we find this to be a place where sadness and joy originate, and all the tools to transmute our sadness, pain, guilt or worry, can be found within this House as well. We would work with acknowledging the sadness, fear etc, and using the breath, begin to breath into the emotions as we anoint ourselves and allow for any tears, crying etc. to flow, releasing the emotions from the core of our being.

The glands and organs that are influenced in this House are, the diaphragm, breath, the adrenal glands, the skin, digestive system, pancreas, gall bladder, liver, and the central nervous system. The upper lumbar and lower thoracic regions of the spine are most associated with this House. Again, when any of the emotional symptoms begin to manifest here, we would want to work on bringing this House back into balance so that the spine, glands and organs do not become affected by the imbalance.

When this House is balanced the outward manifestation of behavior exemplifies one who has their personal will in alignment with their spiritual will. They will radiate acceptance, warmth, and peace from the very center of their being. They will bring cheerfulness and friendliness to all of their talents and expression. When this House is empowered, we will begin to notice a level of spontaneity, and a genuine love of new challenges, and an ability to bring nurturing to themselves and others.

Without balance in this House, some of the more noticeable characteristics and outward behaviors would be depression, lack of confidence, fear of being alone, poor digestion, jealousy and mistrust. Often this imbalance will lead to a propensity for addictions, workaholics, alcoholism, sexual addiction, and or drugs. When any of these symptoms are left untreated for any length of time, we start to witness a deeper imbalance within the glands and organs associated with this House, such as digestive disorders, shortness of breath, liver, gall bladder or spleen dysfunction, nervous disorders, and possible mal-alignment in the upper lumbar or lower thoracic regions of the spine, and if left untreated will continue to manifest into more serious health issues.

Sound Therapy

When strolling through this House singing or toning the ancient sound of OHM (as in OM), a healing resonance vibrates throughout the entire House. The note of A also resonates the highest with this House. When using tuning forks the combination of C and A seem to empower this House the most favorably.

The bija mantra used for this energy center is the mantra of Ram.

When practicing mantra recitation here in this House, you would want to repeat the mantra in a pattern of 3, or a 3 beat rhythm, Ram, Ram, Ram to be most effective.

Crystals and Gemstones

In the magical kingdom of crystals and gemstones, we would seek out the wisdom and collective power of amber. Its name denotes the richness of its color, dark, rich yellow and gold, like the amber colored leaves of autumn.

Amber is actually not a crystal but a fossilized resin of long extinct pine trees that flourished 40-60 million years ago. It carries a rich, morphogenetic wisdom, passed down through millions of years. Amber was one of the crystals to exhibit electricity when studied by science, and many stories associate amber with the sun, the source of all life and immortality.

It has been asserted that amber carries a high vibratory rate and can assist in the purification of the body, in addition to balancing the endocrine and digestive systems. Amber has been said to have a profound affect on the adrenal glands. The balancing of the adrenal gland, which resides within this House, assists all other endocrine glands in balancing due to the release of balanced DHEA, the "mother of all hormones" which will then feed and stimulate the entire endocrine system.

Amber can assist in accessing higher levels of awareness and wisdom, as amber helps to welcome Spirit into the seat of knowing, or the House of Transcendence. The rich golden hues of amber attract prosperity and help nourish the desire to create abundance on every level, as well as the ability to manifest that abundance in a material way. Emotionally, amber encourages peacefulness and allows us to develop a deeper level of trust, which is an emotion that lies within the 3rd House.

Skipping in on the trail of amber is the golden colored gemstone citrine. Citrine is in the quartz family and brings with it an enhancement of psychic intuition, assisting in understanding those "gut feelings". Citrine is a great tool to help prevent nightmares and is said to be the guardian of sleep. Citrine helps to bring the 3rd House into alignment by balancing the solar plexus, and all of the associated glands, organs and skeletal structure.

Citrine shines a bright golden ray into the power center of our beings and attracts abundance and prosperity. Citrine helps bring empowerment into the physical being, and our ability to manifest our Earthly needs. Citrine energizes the body and has the ability to cleanse the solar plexus or 3rd House, and imparts a great deal of invigoration to the physical being. Citrine is an excellent stone to use to help overcome depression and fear, which are emotions that are generated and stored in the 3rd House, and is an excellent stone to use when looking to dispel negativity amongst a group.

Rounding out the trinity of gemstones for the House of Transcendence is topaz. The electrifying nature of topaz magnetizes our entire being, so be sure when using topaz to assist in manifestation, that your intentions are crystal clear, because topaz will increase the level of attraction and the ability to create our reality exactly as we dream it. More and more, we must necessitate clarity in our thoughts, words and actions, as what we declare is made manifest much more quickly than ever before.

Topaz works with the energy meridians of the body, clearing blocks and encouraging an open flow of energy throughout the pathways of the body. It is said to therefore tonify the nerves of the body and enhance the metabolism.

Topaz has also been said to magnetize warmth and love unto us, assisting our ability to stay in present moment awareness, and when focusing on the present allows for a release of our past, enabling us to move beyond fear, guilt, and worry, which is almost always based on the past or future, rarely on the present.

Topaz carries a strong vibration of hope, and replaces fear with optimism and raises us into the Spirit of joy. Topaz has been said to emanate a healing balm into the circulatory system, and induce states of relaxation to combat insomnia.

Essential Oils

The family of essential aromatics has many to choose from when looking to work with the House of Transcendence, but one of the three more notable oils for this House is the resplendent oil of ginger, Zingiber officinalis.

Ginger is an herbaceous perennial that hails from tropical regions around the world. This essential oil has peppery, spicy, lemony, and sensual notes, and has been known to be a boost to the digestive system and circulatory system. Ginger in many different forms, has been used for years in various healing traditions to help settle the stomach and all associated digestive disorders. The tea of ginger has been used to warm the circulatory system as well as aid the digestive systems, and can be used to heat the body during cold winters.

The Egyptians, Greeks, and Romans all considered ginger prized for its effectiveness and some even considered it sacred.

Ginger, when inhaled can be quite stimulating and has long been valued for its aphrodisiacal properties. For centuries, throughout Asia and the South Pacific, ginger was a part of love rituals.

Ginger promotes courage, confidence, and determination, all valuable steps in manifestation. Ginger was once considered more valuable than gold, and is a powerful oil to inhale when visualizing abundance and prosperity. As well, it can be used to anoint for ceremonies to enhance the creation of abundance, and is particularly powerful when blended with frankincense and patchouli.

Ginger is a powerful antiseptic and astringent and should never be applied undiluted or "neat". When mixed in a base oil of jojoba or olive, ginger is a wonderful essential oil to apply to the 3rd House, the chakra of purpose. It can also be used diluted with a carrier oil to warm the extremities of the body when chilled, and to increase the circulation of the blood.

Another delightful aromatic is lemon, Citrus limon. With its fresh, clean, crisp and lively scent, lemon is cheerful and uplifting making it extremely useful for inhalation when working to dispel fear, negativity, and depression.

The essential oil of lemon, like that of orange, is pressed from the outer rind of the lemon. Lemon water, (water with the juice of fresh lemon) has long been a tonic to the digestive system and has been used to purify water due to its high anti-bacterial properties.

When using the essential oil for inhalation (which can be done with a diffuser, or by simply pouring a few drops into the palms of the hands and rubbing the palms together, then cupping the hands around the nose and inhaling deeply) the refreshing essence will bring about an uplifting joyousness to the system. Its lively scent will also assist in activating the body and bringing clarity and energy to the system. Lemon will help to balance this House and build power, particularly when combined with ginger.

The powerful scent of lemon revitalizes and stimulates the central nervous system, enlivening this House while permeating it with purity.

Lemon is a powerful antiseptic and disinfectant, and should not be applied neat to the skin, and in fact, may be caustic to the bare skin, and has been known to cause photosensitivity. Lemon can also be used to disinfect kitchen counters, wood chopping blocks and any surfaces where germs or microbes may linger due to its anti-bacterial, anti-septic and anti-microbial properties.

Lemongrass, Cymbopogon citratus, is another cornerstone of essential oils in this House. The essential oil is distilled from the fresh or dried wild grasses that grow commercially in India, Sri Lanka, Indonesia, Africa, the West Indies, and tropical North and South Americas.

Lemongrass has a long history of use in Ayurvedic medicine where it is prescribed as an antidote to infectious virus or high fever. The enticingly warm, lemony, and grass-like aroma has also been called fevergrass due to its ability to reduce fevers. Lemongrass has remarkable antiseptic and antibacterial properties.

Lemongrass assists greatly with the balancing of the solar plexus and equalizes this seat of fire. Lemongrass helps us with the digestion of new ideas, and when inhaled helps to stimulate psychic awareness, and has also been reported to assist with the regeneration of connective tissue.

Lemongrass has a relaxing effect on the digestive system and is purifying for the body, mind and spirit. As we seek to transcend our fear, worry, guilt and general discomfort with the physical body, and bring about the balancing, activating and awakening of this House, lemongrass will allow us to transcend our emotions and move into the heart, allowing more love into our lives. Lemongrass is a great tonic for the body, mind and spirit, and is one of the more powerful oils for balancing the solar plexus.

Anointing the House of Transcendence

When creating an anointing blend for the House of Transcendence we might want to make sure that our altar is set-up, and again, we would create the anointing oils on either the new moon or full moon. We could have yellow foods placed on the altar to invite the yellow colors to be imbued into the oils that we create to help balance and align this House. We could also have the above-mentioned crystals laid upon the altar to help imbue the chrism with the characteristics of the gemstones, as well as golden candles, pictures etc.

If we are creating an array of different blends for the entire body and each of the Houses, we could include items of color, food, crystals, gemstones, and candles corresponding to each different House of the body. Regardless, we would want to have the candles on the altar lit, fresh flowers for an offering, and a quiet, peaceful environment to blend the oils in.

With our one ounce glass bottle, we would then begin to pour lemongrass first, followed by ginger and finishing with the oil of lemon, constituting at least 28 drops of essential oils to one ounce of pure organic jojoba oil, or for short term use (a maximum of 6 months, stored in a cool dark place) organic olive oil.

After dispensing the essential oils, then finish filling the bottle with the carrier oil of choice, cap the bottle and take it between the palms, rubbing it briskly back and forth, all the while invoking the presence and sanctification of the Divine into the anointing oils. After a few moments, check the oil to make sure that all of the oils have emulsified into one unique anointing chrism. Continue to invoke the presence of the Divine and hold the oils within your palms concentrating the intention into the bottle.

At the time of the anointing, set up a massage table in front of the altar, and have the person being anointed lie down upon the table, or if anointing ourselves, we could sit or lie down in front of the altar.

When it is time to be used for a ceremony, you can then take the anointing blend and drop 5-8 drops into the palm of the hand and apply directly to the House of Transcendence, massaging the oils into the area of the solar plexus. We could also anoint the area of the lumbar region of the spine. Then hold the hand on top of the area for a few minutes until the oils are absorbed into the skin. Often times, when massaging oils into this area of the body, the digestive system becomes quite stimulated, this is a good sign, as it is moving energy, or dissolving energetic blocks in that House. The body can become quite uncomfortable and even experience great pain as energetic blocks get broken up, old anger gets released from the liver or areas of withholding are released in this House. Again, this is an area that tends to hold a lot of pain and emotional blocks, and when releasing that energy, great emotional release can occur along with powerful kriyas moving through the solar plexus region. Hold the area until it quiets, or until any tears or crying have subsided, and then we can choose the appropriate gemstone from the altar to lay upon the body, holding it in place and asking for the color ray of that stone to move through the crystal and into the body in the area of the 3rd House. Visualize golden light pouring into the solar plexus filling it completely. We would then be ready to move onto the tuning forks or toning for this area.

We can strike the notes on the tuning forks and then aim the ends of the tuning forks directly into the House of Transcendence, and or, circle the tuning forks above that area, as it will directly affect the auric field of the solar plexus, helping to align and balance this area. We can also hold the tuning forks about 6 inches away from the ears so the sound is carried through the auditory system balancing the emotional centers of the brain.

We can also tone the sound of OM here, or chant the bija mantra of Ram.

If we are anointing ourselves, we can tone the sounds, or chant the mantra and focus the sound into our bellies, vibrating that chakra into balance.

Again, the combination of oils is affected greatly by the sound vibrations, as well as the power of the gemstones on the body, and each modality will be greatly enhanced by the presence of the other.

When all activity has quieted in that region, we can then move onto the next House or sit quietly with that House and allow for the activation and balance to be completed, giving thanks for the presence of the Divine and the consecration of that House as holy.

Chapter 6

The House of Heart

Temple of Love

And think not you can direct

The course of love,

For love,

If it finds you worthy,

Directs your course.

Kahlil Gibran

Welcome home to the House of Heart, the deepest seat of love and compassion, and center of our truest essential self. The House of Heart lies in the very center of our being, the heart chakra and is the place where we are most inclined to find Spirit.

The yogic term used to identify this heart center is the anahata, and it is the place where the physical merges with the spiritual, and a place where the emotions of love and hate are most deeply felt. The heart is also the place where the deepest level of compassion resides, and where the conscious and the subconscious merge together, melt into the fires of love and send a spiraling wave of love back out through the entire body ascending and descending through the body with the healing light of compassionate loving.

When we seek to move further along the path of compassionate loving, it is always important to look at our reasons for compassion and how we work with compassion. Compassion is the deep awareness and sympathy for another's suffering. It is very easy for us to use compassion as a means of manipulation or for attention. It is also very easy to slip into compassion with an attachment to the outcome. We grow through all levels of compassion, and the hope is to come to a place within our selves whereupon we are able to practice detached compassion, allowing our selves to feel compassion and loving support for our fellow human, but without a desire to change any outcome.

When we begin to practice compassion with love and detachment, we are allowing for the highest possible outcome, knowing that each individual involved in the experience is gaining something quite necessary albeit sometimes painful in their soul's evolution. We can only hope to know what words or actions are appropriate for our own experience; each and every other person on the planet has a soul that directs their experience for the highest possible outcome. When we can begin to understand that each soul is learning from a particular experience, we can start to trust their soul knows exactly what they are doing when creating circumstances that involve great suffering. Although its hard to watch those we love suffer, when we move out of judgment and recognize that soul as absolute Divine perfection, we can practice compassion for the suffering while offering loving support for their experience.

If we trace back the emergence of the seven major religious traditions during the Axial Age, 900 to 200 BCE, we can see that during those years the different traditions were seeking new visions for humanity to lead people from the violence that was predominate at that time. The core common belief amongst all those religions during that time was a belief that the only way one could encounter what they called God, Brahman, Nirvana, or the Way, was to live a compassionate life.

Our task today amidst the chaos and violence prevalent in our world is to overcome our selfishness and egotism, and learn to live in a compassionate manner, or as the Golden Rule states, "Do unto others as you would have done unto you". If we can all learn to sit in the seat of our compassionate hearts and offer love and support to one another, regardless of race or religion, we are well on our way of ensuring the survival of this species. It is time to see the Brahman in everyone we meet, and treat one another, as we would like to be treated.

Compassion can be one of our greatest teachers when desiring to expand into unconditional loving. There must be a continual surrender of judgment and deep opening of the heart to move into the state of unconditional love. When we practice anointing the House of Heart regularly, we are able to assist our hearts opening to deeper levels of awareness, love and non-judgment, allowing for a compassionate loving way of being in the world, without conditions or limits.

This House sits in the very center of our chests, including the heart, the area, in and around the 1st thoracic vertebra and the thymus gland. The House of Heart is awash in both deep emerald green and or, opalescent golden pink, and these colors are most significant for this House, providing the most balance and harmonizing for the home of our hearts.

The angels of color are always more than eager to assist with the invocation of color to aid in balancing and healing this part of our body and soul. When asking the angels to assist, the following invocation just serves as an example of an invocation that could be used to ask for the assistance of the Elohim or the angelic keepers of color to bring forth their healing rays.

Invocation to the Emerald Green Ray

I call upon the Elohim of the Emerald Green Ray,
To pour your verdant color into my House of Heart.
Envelope my heart with your abundant emerald color,
And allow me the full surrender of Love.
Lush, emerald green ray
Spill forth through all of my body, carry love
Through every part of my being,
Align, balance and spiral into the very center of my heart,
Awaken me to the ecstasy of love.

The House of Heart follows the seventh direction of the medicine wheel, within, and the mystic who lives here can truly say, "I love Spirit, Source, Brahman, God, or the Divine with all my heart and soul, I recognize myself as that and I love and recognize my fellow human as myself." The direction of within is the place in Native American culture where we come to truly know Spirit, to feel Spirit and the warm embrace of Divine Love. All of the vision quests were taken with the intention of going deep inside the heart to find Source, and therein the answers to any and all questions.

The Hindus call this path bhakti yoga, the way of devotion. Bhakti is the Sanskrit term that signifies a blissful, selfless and overwhelming love of God or the Divine, and sees that Divine everywhere and in all things.

We can be devoted to a particular deity or aspect of the Divine such as God, (Krishna, Yahweh, Allah and there are many more names for the same thing,) but when we begin to see with the eyes of the heart, we can begin to see and respect the Divine in every person, and in all things. This devotion comes from living from the heart and immersing our selves into the love and compassion that holds court here in the heart center, or the 4th chakra, and is perfected through some form of daily devotional practice, be it the practice of yoga, meditation, prayer, chanting, seva (the act of self-less service), spending time with advanced spiritual teachers or gurus, or other deeply spiritual practices.

It is in this fourth heart center that the thymus gland resides, and within Eastern thought the thymus gland represents the boundary between heaven (the three topmost Houses) and Earth, (the three lower Houses). The six-pointed star is the representative icon from the Hindu culture that is used to symbolize the merger of heaven and Earth that occurs in the House of Heart.

This symbol is also called the Star of David, the Shield of David, or the Magen Davi, and is generally the recognized symbol of the Jewish Community. It was named after King David, and its usage began in the Middle Ages. According to some, it represents seven points, with the center being the seventh point, again, a symbolic representation of the merger of heaven and Earth that occurs within the center, or the heart region.

We travel to this House when we seek clarity of truth and inspiration, for it is in the centered heart of love, that we find access to all wisdom and illumination of the Divine. One of the more celebrated paths to love is through the practice of compassion. In order to fully understand the wisdom of compassion we must first begin to become compassionate with our selves. The ability to feel compassion is one of the mystic's paths on the road to love. The other path that is traveled to reach the innermost dwelling place of love within the House of Heart is the path of forgiveness. Learning to forgive brings us much closer to living in the center of our love for longer and longer periods of time.

Now, forgiveness can be a funny thing, as it is so often the case that we can forgive others much more readily than we can forgive our selves, and it is there we must begin, for if we cannot forgive our selves, the path to the center of our heart does not become illuminated.

The true path of forgiveness lies not so much in the ability to forgive what we tend to perceive as poor behavior in our selves or others, but rather, forgiveness is a call to responsibility. Taking responsibility for our word and our actions allows us to really examine our motives and the reason we say and do things. If someone becomes angry or hurt as a result of our words or actions, it is in the responsibility that we take for the pain or suffering where we begin to grow and transform our inner drives and motivations. In forgiving our selves we embark upon the journey from suffering guilt for something we have done (or not done) to celebrating the process of transformation that occurs within the heart as we acknowledge that we are growing and becoming more loving, more compassionate, and more caring.

The transformation of the heart can only come about when we

realize that the results of our actions or words may sometimes have had a less desirable outcome than we had hoped, which then allows us to begin a reflection on those results, and as we begin to look deeper to find the motivation for our actions, we can heal any misguided motivation and allow our selves the space to grow and choose more appropriately in the future. The heart then moves into a celebration of transformation, and love is unleashed, not only for our selves, but also for the lessons we learn along the way. It is through this process we start to fall deeply into the state of love, where all bliss, ecstasy and joy reside.

One of the greatest ways to maintain illumination and devotion to the House of Heart is through the active daily practice of meditation or prayer. One of the great gifts of building an altar for anointing is that we can use that altar daily to sit and re-connect through our devotional practices of prayer and mediation.

When we continually return to the altar, and the adjacent area around the altar, an amazing thing begins to happen. That area begins to exude a holy and sacred energy, and by continually anointing and practicing, that area begins to become a place where every time we sit, if even for a moment, we become touched by the energy of the sacred, the energy of the Divine that permeates the very air surrounding the altar.

When we go deep into prayer and meditation, we journey deep into our heart, the seat of our soul, and the home to our Divine nature and we are reminded of the truism, we are *spiritual* beings, having a human experience. When we remind ourselves of that truth again, and again, we begin to live, think, speak and act with the knowledge that we are Spirit in a body, and our daily lives begin to become more sacred, holy, and Divine.

By actively declaring an intention to stay seated upon the lotus throne of our heart, we are affirming our commitment to live in a conscious loving and compassionate manner, and our experiences in life begin to reflect that back to us.

In other words, when we focus our attention on the heart, and regularly visit that House, we bring love into all that we think, say, do and aspire to do. What a glorious way to unify and heal the wounds of humanity that have held us slaves to separation for such a long time.

The organs and glands that make their home here are the

heart, the lungs, (which are organs that carry emotion as well as the organs that store grief), the immune system, the thymus gland, the lymph system, the arms and hands, and the circulatory system. These glands and organs are fed by the color, vitamins and minerals of the following foods, salads, asparagus, cucumbers, green apples, kiwi, celery, leeks, chives, limes and cherimoyas. These foods all help to regenerate, refresh, and re-balance this House and all the resident organs, glands and systems that reside here.

Music and song are one of the best ways to open this House and raise the windows of the heart and soul. Songs in the key of F# particularly resonate here, along with the tone of AH or AUM, sometimes sung as OM. When toning this sacred chant, focus our intention to send vibration of the sound into the heart area and it is quite possible to feel the resonance as the sound vibrates in this energy center. The tuning forks you would want to use to balance the House of Heart would be C and A.

The bija mantra chanted to activate balance and harmony in this House is the mantra of Yam, usually chanted in a four beat rhythm. Chanting this mantra during meditation is a great way to bring illumination and clarity to the House of Heart. Also singing and dancing will lift the vibratory frequency of the heart, and will bring us into the state of joy. Mother Teresa had her orphans dance 20 minutes a day, as it was her belief that if we danced 20 minutes a day, we would always be happy.

This House will most assuredly be in balance when we demonstrate an openness and vitality in our personality, signifying a heart-based harmony. When the heart is balanced, energy flows openly throughout the body, and there is a feeling of fullness and contentment that emanates out into the world for all to see and partake. Our hearts become so full of love it begins to radiate out from the heart, and people will be naturally drawn to us, often not even knowing why we are so attractive. When there is perfect balance and contentment in the heart, our tendency is to radiate love and compassion, and to see the good in all things and all situations.

A deficiency or imbalance in this House manifests itself with characteristic indecisiveness, fear of surrender, fear of abandonment, and general low self esteem. Heart problems tend to manifest with an imbalance here, showing up in the physical as cardiac problems, and in the emotional as moodiness or depression. Deficiencies in the thymus gland will also manifest if this House is left unbalanced for any length of time.

Martyrs also tend to develop well within the House of Heart if there is an imbalance left unattended. The emotional symptoms are often our first clue that something is not right within this House, and are much more easily addressed than physical symptoms, as the physical body is the densest of all the bodies we have and hence the hardest to deal with in terms of clearing, healing and balancing. The spiritual body is the lightest and easiest to address, the emotional body would be next, the mental a little more involved, and the body the last to resolve imbalance.

Another really important function of meditation can be to help us stay in touch with the energetic body, and the first inklings of something being off in our system. If we can address any issues of imbalance in this lighter energetic field, we have a much easier time reconciling the energy body, before it begins to affect our emotions, and then eventually our body.

It is said, and from experience we know this to be true, that the body never lies, we can rationalize and make excuses in our minds for our conditions, but the body will always tell us the truth. Once a problem has manifested in our physical bodies, it becomes necessary to make a more radical change to bring about harmony in the body, the emotional system, the mental body, and finally the energetic body of the Spirit. If we can become masters of our energetic bodies, we can save our physical bodies much in the way of non-health and disease.

Meditation is a tool to help us stay in touch with the subtle aspects of our being, and we can then do the work on the subtle bodies before it manifests into physical discomfort.

It's always a good idea to practice self-inquiry on a regular basis to determine where we might be in a state of imbalance within any of our bodies, and learn to see the energetic bodies and when they might be in a state of need. If we can address imbalances within those bodies first, then we can often avoid problems before they manifest in the physical body, in the form of heart disease, circulatory conditions, lung disease, or problems with the endocrine system.

Gemstones and Crystals

There are many useful tools to help bring balance and alignment to this heart center, and one of the more powerful allies to the House of Heart is certainly the rose quartz crystal.

Rose quartz assists in attracting love to this House and helps love radiate throughout the entire body, mind, and spirit. The soft, vibrational quality of rose quartz has a soothing effect on any irregularities within the heart. The soft opalescent, pink rays of love are attracted to and embody this beauty, illuminating the House of Heart with its lovely radiance. Rose quartz brings balance and integration to the polarized aspects of the yin and yang within our heart, allowing for unification of our masculine and feminine aspects.

Rose quartz amplifies feelings of self-love with a gentleness reflective of the soft hues of its coloring, and gentle loving vibration, and empowers the act of forgiveness and compassion. Rose quartz is a powerful ally to enlist when seeking to empower our hearts with the cornerstones of forgiveness and compassion on the pathway home to the center of our soul, the heart. Rose quartz carries the vibration of unconditional love and imbues the heart with the true essence of love. Rose quartz is an excellent stone to use on the altar or in the bedroom to attract love or relationship into our lives.

Rose quartz teaches us forgiveness, the ultimate tool on the path of unconditional love. It teaches us about self-love and self-acceptance and encourages healing when dealing with a broken heart or emotional trauma.

Rhodocrosite is mystically linked with the House of Heart in its ability to inspire love. Rhodocrosite has been said to vibrate our consciousness into spiritual awareness, celebrating the reception of higher forms of wisdom into our hearts. Rhodocrosite is a powerful stone capable of reinforcing our auric field with radiant protective light, and assists our ability to stay seated in the jewel of our heart.

Rhodocrosite is an excellent stone to work with when working on children, as it seems to have a natural affinity to the purity and carefree heart of a child. Generally it is this kind of attitude that supports the most gentle immersion of our selves into love. Rhodocrosite is a natural choice when looking to deepen the love of self. Rhodocrosite stimulates the growth of self worth and soothes emotional hurt, thereby bringing about a stronger sense of our true worth. It is also a stone to be used when looking to lift depression.

Another magical wizard who loves to come and play with the heart is kunzite. Kunzite is a lavender pink jewel that has been declared a protector of children's souls. Kunzite contains within it, lithium, and as such, some maintain its ability to soften the House of Heart, allowing for a deeper expansion of Spirit into physical form.

It has been claimed also, that kunzite helps with penetrating emotional blocks in the heart and allows for an opening to deeper levels of loving.

Kunzite helps to integrate and balance polarization of the masculine and feminine. Kunzite brings with its bevy of magical properties, a balance to body, mind and spirit, with its representation of true light and the color of love.

Kunzite awakens the House of Heart and allows for a deeper understanding of unconditional love and the compassionate path that brings us to that understanding. Kunzite will encourage humility and is helpful in reducing stress in the heart. It is an excellent stone to use when looking to alleviate panic attacks or any other stress related anxiety.

Essential Oils

Green myrtled isle where flowers lushly grow,
The quenchless source of all men's veneration,
Where sighs from hearts consumed by adoration
Drift, like the scent of roses as they blow.

Baudelaire

In the world of adoration, the rose has long been the symbol of a true love's ardor and expression. Rose, Rosa damascena, is one of the most sacred and powerful essential oils and is said to have been one of the seven sacred oils to the ancient Egyptians, and was venerated by the Greeks and Romans as well. Roses have been prized throughout the history of time and have long been the very symbol of love itself. There is no praise great enough to herald the beauty and intoxicating aroma of a pure rose essential oil. Pure rose oil vibrates at the highest measurable frequency, the frequency of love and when inhaled will actually induce pink color into the aura, (if we could ascribe a color to love, it would be pink).

The essential oil comes from the petals of the rose, which must be hand picked, preferably picked with the morning dew still upon the petals so that the oil has not begun to evaporate into the heat of the morning sun. It requires 60,000 of these hand picked rosebuds to produce one ounce of essential oil. It is certainly easy to gain perspective and understanding about the extraordinary expense of this beloved oil. The finest rose oil comes from Bulgaria and Turkey, but is also grown in other parts of the world as well.

The rose is a native of the Orient, but is now grown more or less all over the world, mainly in temperate climates. The Romans made lavish use of roses: they scattered them from the ceilings during their festivals, and adorned their statues of the Gods with rose boughs. The Greeks also venerated the rose, with Homer eulogizing it in the Iliad and the Odyssey, and Sappho dubbing it the queen of all flowers. The Egyptians used roses in religious ceremonies and many mummies were found buried with roses.

Rose oil is divinely sweet, rich and deeply floral, with herbal undertones and although it is known for its fragrance, the flower actually has very little aromatic oil, hence the need for such a large amount of plant material.

The Arabic physician Avicenna, who wrote an entire book on the many healing properties of rose, was the first to distill the essential oil of rose. Rose oil is a gentle tonic for the heart, and is gentle enough to be used neat (undiluted) on the skin. Rose is an excellent choice to balance and soothe the emotions and for inspiring romantic feelings, in addition to the physical balancing qualities it brings to the heart.

Rose has a long history of use in the aromatic world of perfumery, being one of the main constituents in some of the top perfumes made in the world today. Rose oil has long been included in skin care preparations as well, due to the excellent moisturizing properties of the oil and the amazing cell regenerative properties.

Rose oil, because it resonates closest to the vibration of love, is an excellent friend to invite into the House of Heart. Rose oil with its soft, herbal, sweet, floral notes has an instant uplifting effect and is a supreme oil that will induce love and joy into the heart.

Due to its alluring capacity to attract love, rose oil has long been used as an aphrodisiac and a major ingredient in all love potions. Rose oil is also said to help balance the female hormones and has been used to bring about regularity in monthly cycles. Rose is stimulating to the sexual center of the body, in addition to the emotional qualities of love within the heart. Rose oil is the supreme oil when looking to bring about activation, healing, balance and inspiration to the heart.

A Rose by any other name would hardly smell as sweet.

The oil of the angels descends next, angelica, Angelica archangelica officinalis. Angelica creates a cocoon of celestial protection around the House of Heart, and invokes the angelic helpers with our ascent into love.

The essential oil of angelica comes from the roots of a plant native to Europe and Syria. The angelica plant is a furry plant with ferny leaves and umbels of white flowers. It has a very peppery, musky and Earthy smell upon inhalation and induces a state of warmth and relaxation. Angelica grows up to 6 feet tall and it takes 340 pounds of plant material to produce one pound of essential oil.

Known as the "holy Spiritroot", or "oil of angels", angelica's healing powers were considered to be so strong as to be thought of as Divine. The fragrance when inhaled has been known to help in releasing negative emotions and releasing grief, and can also be calming and soothing to the heart.

Angelica is an excellent oil to use when looking to aid someone recovering from an emotional trauma with its natural ability to release negative trauma from the cellular system. Angelica also carries the ability to reinforce the auric field with the protective energy of the angelic forces. Angelica basically invokes the aid of the angels in creating a protective field around our bodies, and has a very calming affect on the central nervous system, and also strengthens the emotional body. Angelica is one of the most powerful oils to use when working with prayers of forgiveness during any kind of healing from the emotional grief of a broken heart.

Angelica assists in attracting the golden ray of celestial light and anchoring it firmly in the heart center, opening us to the heart of the Divine within. Angelica is a superior oil to use when looking to empower self-love, as it is an incredible spiritual healer for the heart.

The essential oil of geranium, Pelargonium graveolens is a very nurturing oil that carries the essence of the Divine Mother. The oil of geranium has a rich, green rose-like aroma. The oil is produced from the flowers, leaves and stems of the perennial shrub.

Geranium is a general tonic and sedative for the entire central nervous system and an excellent skin care oil due to its anti-inflammatory properties, soothing the nerves of the skin. Geranium also has wonderful antiseptic, anti-viral and anti-bacterial properties as well, making it an excellent tonic for the skin.

Geranium, the oil of the Divine Mother awakens us to the deep, nurturing mother love in our hearts, the feminine aspect that so wants to nurture our selves and others. As such, it is an excellent choice for assisting others through grief and trauma due to the loss of a loved one.

Geranium helps to alleviate the effects of exhaustion and is a wonderful anti-depressant. The oil of geranium is astonishing for protecting children while they sleep. Place a few drops in the palm of the hand and then rub along the spine of the child, (no more than three drops) and there will be a protective field set up around the child, as if sleeping in the arms of their mother.

The oil of geranium is a valuable oil to choose when looking to activate an awakening within the House of Heart, persuading love to grow and permeate our being, reconciling us with the innermost sanctum of our selves, the part of our selves that is Divine LOVE.

Dr. Malte Hozzel, the founder of Oshadi essential oils, says, "Geranium's vital, sensual presence is not subtle, but direct and unavoidable, making it one of the oils of choice for aphrodisiac qualities. Geranium inspires natural beauty & enjoyment, uplifts instantly & tonifies the mind & intellect in a powerful, nearly demanding attitude".

Geranium, when mixed with angelica and rose oil, are powerful allies of the heart and invite love in to dance.

Anointing the House of Heart
Seated in front of the altar with candles lit, flowers laid upon the altar, take the prescribed essential oils and begin by pouring

geranium into a one ounce bottle, followed by angelica, and then rose oil, using the prescribed amount from previous chapters. Fill the remainder of the bottle with the choice of carrier oil, and cap. All the while we are mixing the oil, we can be invoking the presence of the Divine into the anointing chrism, and asking that the prescribed chrism be filled with the power to activate, integrate and balance the House of Heart.

Once the bottle is full, cap the top and then take the anointing blend between our two palms and rub briskly back and forth allowing all of the oils to emulsify together. Ask for the presence of the Divine to be infused into the anointing oils, consecrating them and allowing them to become sacred. If blending on the full moon, then take the anointing chrism outside and allow it to be bathed by the moonlight for a few hours or overnight, being careful to bring the oils in before the sun comes up, as sunlight can altar the frequency and power of the oils. When storing our anointing blends, we will always want to keep them out of sunlight, avoid temperatures above 95 degrees, and away from electrical appliances to maintain the electrical frequency of the oils.

We could then place the anointing chrism onto the altar and leave it there for any length of time allowing the energy of our altar to also be infused within the chrism.

When it is time to anoint the House of Heart, again, light the candles on the altar, offer a prayer of thanks to the Divine for assisting in bringing harmony to the anointing oils and allowing them the full expression of sacred consecration. Invite the presence of all the angels, masters, teachers and guides that dwell in the highest realms of love to be present and pour their love down into us and to aid and assist in any way so that the anointing be for the highest possible good.

Take the anointing chrism for the House of Heart and pour 5-6 drops of oil into the palm of the hand, then dipping a finger into the oils, begin to massage the oils onto the heart, from the area above the diaphragm, all the way up to the sternum. Hold the hand over the skin once the oil has been applied and begin to invoke and visualize an emerald green ray, infused with opalescent pink light into the oils, penetrating the oils into the House of Heart. Hold the hand on the body for a minimum of 4-5 minutes, long enough for the oils to penetrate the skin and enter the bloodstream.

If healing emotional grief or sadness, there may be an emotional release of tears, or sobbing that is initiated with the application of the chrism. Allow for the release to manifest and clear before moving the hand away. This combination of essential oils can be very powerful for releasing old trauma and wounds from the heart. As someone is releasing any level of grief or trauma, it is important to keep a hand on the heart, to help hold him or her in an aura of protection for the entire trauma to leave the body through the tears, or sobs. It is also quite comforting to place the other hand on top of the head to help ground the body through the process of release. Once the release is complete (crying etc. has stopped, kriyas are no longer moving through the body etc.), visualize love and emerald light pouring into the heart, and see the area above the heart filled with light as well.

Retrieve the chosen crystal from the altar and place it in the center of the heart, again, invoking the healing colors to move through the gemstone into the heart center, amplifying the power of the oils that have now absorbed into the body.

At this point in time, we would take the tuning forks C and A, and lightly sound them, and direct the healing sound vibrations into the heart. We would also want to wave the tuning forks above the body, allowing the sound to vibrate through the energetic body of the House of Heart and also hold the forks close to the ear (at least 6 inches away) to allow the sound to move through the auditory system as well.

The Heart Math Institute in Northern California has discovered that the energetic field radiating away from the body in the area of the heart, actually extends at least eight feet around and in front of the body, giving credence to the old saying, "She wears her heart on her sleeve".

In actuality, the energy of our hearts extends out away from the body for quite some distance. Due to the technical limitations of their current equipment, their studies have shown the energetic field to expand out at least 8 feet from the physical body, but they believe with more advanced technology, we are going to find that the energetic field of the heart actually extends much farther than that. If indeed, the research of the quantum physicists proves that there is a "living mind of God" that exists everywhere, than the heart extends infinitely into the Universe, and we are indeed all connected through our hearts, which is the seat of our soul.

We could chant or tone the sound of AUM or OM at this point, vibrating the sound into our own heart, or holding our mouths over the person we are anointing and directing the sound into their House of Heart. We could also chant the bija mantra of Yam at this point as well. Allow for a full immersion into love at this point, feel it filling the body, or the body of the one being anointed, and allow everything to disappear into love. Feel the warmth of love overwhelming the entire body, filling the mind and emotional body and allow the mind to disappear completely into the state of love. The House of Heart should be filled with delicious, sweet warmth, and the intoxicating aromas of the anointing blend should be wafting throughout the temple of love.

We could then direct our attention on to the throat chakra, or the House of Growth, our temple of communication. If we were only anointing the heart, then we would want to sit quietly in meditation, focusing our healing intentions into the House of Heart, allowing for a continued expansion of love throughout that House and the entire body.

Chapter 7

The House of Growth

Temple of Communication

Smells are surer

Than sights and sounds

To make your heartstrings sing.

Rudyard Kipling

When we step over the threshold and enter into the inner sanctum of the House of Growth, it is a remembrance that we are entering into a pledge of honest and forthright truth, a vow that honors the temple of communication. The 5th House is the center of our vocal expression and the place where we initiate communication with others.

This is the House that allows for the expansion of love that occurs in the House of Heart to be expressed truthfully and completely, without hesitation and is also called the throat chakra.

The House of Growth occupies the direction of the north on the Native American medicine wheel. The north holds host to the season of winter, and during the season of winter we are most inclined to hibernate, go within, slow down, rest, and find our truth. When we share stories and communicate after a period of quiet reflection, it comes from a place of honest expression.

It is therefore advisable to "think before we speak", allow ourselves a moment of quiet reflection to discover the honest expression of truth before responding in communication. Most often, our tendency is to speak from the intellectual or emotional response, rather than reflect on a statement and really go inside to find the resonant spiritual truth before speaking a response. Taking just a few moments to reflect before speaking is a powerful way to begin a much more intimate form of communication. Deep reflection before speaking is a touchstone to carry with us as we continue to work towards conscious communication.

It is through conscious communication, that we can use the love from the House of Heart, and express it through the House of Growth, the throat chakra, as we look to deepen the relationships that were initiated in the House of Water, our 2nd chakra.

The 5th House represents discipline, responsibility, and will, and in Hindu philosophy is the way of raja yoga, the union of the Divine through the practice of a moral discipline that preserves the tribe or the community, honors life, and leads to personal growth.

In yogic terms, it is called the vishudda, and is intimately connected with the thyroid gland and all manners of communication. It is through conscious communication we become able to deepen and preserve the relationships we build with our tribe.

When the will is strongly focused through a discipline such as meditation or prayer, we are capable of using energy co-creatively with the Divine in the manifestation of our dreams. Living a life devoted to spiritual practice, allows for the development of compassion, creativity, healing and service. When we express and communicate from this deep place of reverence, we speak with kindness and love, and the beauty of compassion.

Amongst many of the Eastern traditions there is a practice that encourages vows of silence for periods of time, which enables clear and conscious communication when it's resumed.

Often, if we take the time to sit in silence, if even for a moment, we can return to a place of compassion before we speak and our communications will reflect back to us the beauty of love, rather than communicating from a more reactive response. This study in compassionate expression allows an act of integrity to initiate our interactions with others, and is one of the most powerful ways of communicating through the act of speech.

The path of non-judgment is also a powerful way in which we influence our communication with others, and it is within the House of Growth where we can address the identity of judgment.

Often in the midst of communicating with others, we interpret what people are saying with an emotional attachment or a judgment about what is being said, which can trigger an emotionally reactive response based on some personal fear or inadequacy that gets triggered. When we practice non-judgment we must also stay very aware of our speech, and the thoughts that propel our words to express themselves. If we find ourselves judging something someone says to us negatively, we will almost certainly have an emotion tied up with the judgment. When we speak back to them without taking a moment for consideration; we are controlled by the emotion of our judgment. If we can take a moment and learn to sit inside before responding, we can take the time to look at the judgment, acknowledge it, and discern the emotion behind the judgment. When we practice this before speaking, we can often identify our own emotional issues, and work to heal things within ourselves before responding negatively in comment or action. With practice this can allow us to move into more unbiased and conscious forms of communication, thus helping to cultivate deeper levels of expression within our relationships.

As we continue to choose to look at an idea, experience, or conversation from a more detached place, or from a perspective of non-judgment, (instead of being subjective and vulnerable which could lead to taking things personally), we begin to become much more objective in our responses. By maintaining a more objective stance in life, we can experience life more as a witness, which keeps us from getting involved in the drama which so often causes suffering.

Our forms of communication can then transcend into a form of objective observation and our speech will express compassionate truth, providing another opportunity for us to practice detached compassion, which is also a lesson that comes in the House of Heart. The heart feels compassion without becoming emotionally involved, and therefore can express itself through the throat center without self-righteousness, or the hidden desire to control and manipulate or change the experience of another. Our desire to change anyone else's experience or life is based on an arrogant notion that we are better or know more than someone else in determining what is best for them. Every soul is choosing exactly the right experience that person needs to have in order to grow, change, heal and evolve.

The quantum physicists continue to tell us, we are each a Divine spark of God having an Earthly experience, and as such, we are all perfectly capable of creating the absolute paramount experience we need to have in life in order for our souls to evolve.

The only time when we need to impose our will on another is as a parent when we must do what we think is the most appropriate to keep a child safe and teach them how to live according to the tribal codes. It is the responsibility of a parent to allow the child a safe and completely protected environment in which to grow into their appropriate self-expression.

The House of Growth is awash in the colors of a celestial turquoise blue kingdom of light. The walls are colored a turquoise sky blue, the color of clouds that float on angel wings, reflecting back the bright hues of a summer afternoon.

Invocation to the Celestial Turquoise Blue Ray

I call forth the Elohim of the Celestial Turquoise Blue Ray
To overflow your radiance of blue color and light
Into my fifth House of Growth.
Ocean blue light, Sweeten my voice
Empower my speech with the truth of the Divine.
Celestial turquoise blue ray
Spill forth your color and light, align me with Source,
And radiate through me entire being.

There is an etheric universal energy that pervades this House. When this House is balanced, we are truly at one with our selves in the world, there is an alignment between assertion and Spirit, and we are always inspired by devotion here.

The emotions of serenity and sorrow both call the House of Growth home. It is through the experience of sorrow that our greatest strengths are born, allowing us to slip more easily into serenity. When we are seated firmly in the chair of serenity, we are much more capable of practicing detached compassion and empowering communication with love and peaceful intentions as we continue to deal with sorrow. It is through the experience of sorrow that we truly begin to understand the depth of serenity, they are the polar opposite expressions of the same emotion, and exist to give each other depth and perspective.

It is true with so many of our emotions; they give definition to their opposites. How could we ever know the depths of love, if we did not have the perspective of fear to shine light on the love, fear is the absence of love, and so it is that love melts fear, serenity melts sorrow, happiness melts sadness, etc. etc.

The throat, the thyroid, the hypothalamus, the central nervous system, the mouth, and ears all reside in the House of Growth. The tone of EH (as in pleasure) resonates the highest with all the occupants of this House. When singing, toning or chanting, this tone seems to settle into the throat and vibrate it into balance. The note of G is also particularly stimulating to this House. Singing is a very powerful way to open up the 5th House, and helps free up communication and inquiry into truth based expression.

The bija mantra of Ham in a five beat rhythm could also be chanted here to help empower and bring balance to this House.

When using tuning forks, we would use the C and G forks to help vibrate this House into balance through sound.

When this House is in balance, we will be much more inclined to speak the truth, communicating clearly and easily in a steady, eloquent manner. We will be inspired artistically and musically, which gives rein to creative expression. Here, in a balanced House, we will find integration of peace, truth and knowledge. It is also here in the center of vocal expression that we find the principal of loyalty instigated.

When there is a lack of balance in this House, we find exhibits of timid behavior, fear, an inability to verbalize thoughts and feelings, unreliability, and one who might be prone to feeling uncomfortable in the body. In addition one might also exhibit signs of arrogance, talking for the sake of talking, and self-righteous speech or behavior. These signs are evident to inspire us to begin work to balance and align this House, before it manifests into physical symptoms that might include any kind of sore throat, hoarseness, thyroid imbalance which manifest in the symptoms of easy fatigue, exhaustion for no reason, cold hands and feet, constipation, and if left untreated, will manifest into deeper symptoms of excessive dry skin and hair falling out.

The banquet served to assist in bringing balance to the House of Growth is almost certain to include any or all of the bluish colored foods, blueberries, plums, grapes, prunes, and blue cornmeal.

Crystals and Gemstones

There is an abundance of possibilities in the gemstone world, but there are a few gemstones that have been used traditionally to balance this House and assist with the healing of the symptoms mentioned. One of the most powerful stones used to assist the healing and balancing of the throat, also happens to be the oldest stone in recorded history.

Turquoise is found all over the world, with as many color variations in its form, as locations in which it is found. Turquoise was even mined by the ancient Egyptians, and archeologists have seen astonishing similarities between the carved turquoises found in Egyptian tombs and the pieces found in the gravesites of the North American ancestors. One might even conclude there was clearly a link between the indigenous people of the Earth thousands of years ago.

Native Americans have long believed turquoise to be a powerful stone that would provide protection to the wearer, and it has, and continues to be, used in ceremonial tools and carvings. Hindus believed that to gaze upon the stone of turquoise in the light of the moon, was to insure great luck. In the Middle East, it was believed that turquoise would help to ward off accidents. The Navajos revere turquoise and consider it sacred and holy, believing it to be the heart of Grandmother Earth.

In addition to the protection it provides, turquoise works with the blue ray of wisdom and truth, providing us with the courage to speak our truth. Turquoise will help to release old inhibitions and calm nerves enabling an easier time with communication and vocal expression.

Turquoise helps to balance and align the pituitary gland, enhancing our powers of creative manifestation. It assists with the integration of the cosmic currents and light rays now being broadcast down onto the planet from the angelic realms to awaken higher states of consciousness.

Another stone occasionally found growing alongside turquoise is chrysacolla, and it shares many of the same powers as turquoise. Chrysacolla is a relative with more recent heraldry than turquoise, and many say it is a stone that accompanies the awakening of spiritual remembrance on the Earth.

Chrysacolla is a pleasing, mint blue color, and when laid across the House of Growth, induces feelings of peace and calm, allowing for the clear expression of truth. Chrysacolla evokes visions of autumn seas, harbors of serenity, and empowers comfort in the feeling nature of our being, allowing a deeper expression of truth in our communication. Chrysacolla just seems to strike an accord between the feeling nature of our being and the expressive nature of our being.

Chrysacolla encourages a strong sense of self and inner balance between the clear desire to speak one's truth and a discernment that brings clarity as to when it might be time to remain silent, which allows for sensitive and clear communication.

Chrysacolla and turquoise are equally at home in the House of Growth.

Essential Oils

Resonating regally in this House, we find three powerful essential oils that will help create balance, alignment, and wellness within this temple of communication. Lavender, Lavandula officinalis is one of the most sacred of the oils to the ancient Egyptian cultures. Lavender is a fragrant, flowering evergreen shrub, native to Southern Europe, particularly around the Mediterranean regions and is the most widely used and available essential oil throughout the world. The essential oil is lightly colored, with herbal, sweet, delicate floral notes, and is one of the most powerful healers in the world of essential oils.

The oil is produced from the leaves, flowers, and stems of the plant. On a hot summer's day, you can actually look at the plant and see the oil droplets on the leaves and flowers. When we stand in front of a lavender plant on a warm summer day, with the sun shining behind the plant, we can actually see the oils evaporating into the heat of the sun, creating a natural diffuser, atomizing the air with the clean, sweet, fresh smell of lavender.

Lavender has been used since ancient times as it is a universal oil and contains every conceivable property, antiviral, antibacterial, antiseptic, antibiotic, anti-inflammatory, etc, etc. It is both a relaxant and stimulant depending upon the dosage, and contains every other property as well.

Lavender is *the* essential oil for burns, and is even used in burn wards of some of the hospitals in Europe due to its ability to prevent burns from blistering and scarring.

Lavender is an excellent oil to use when visualizing optimum health and creates an aura of protection around the body, mind, and spirit. Lavender also has the ability to clear away negative energy and enhance clarity, making it an excellent oil to work with the center of our expression, the throat chakra, or the House of Growth.

Lavender promotes deep meditation and assists with all forms of communication. In particular, it is a great boost to the communicative powers of the higher self (or our Divine self) with the conscious mind, enabling our voice to ring with the truth of Spirit.

Lavender is refreshing, and an excellent antidepressant, and when used sparingly, will help promote deep sleep. There have been volumes of literature written about the amazing healing powers of lavender, and it is a friend that is welcome in any House.

Chamomile, Matricaria chamomilla, or German, is another of the sacred oils used in the ancient Egyptian civilizations, and is a star in its own right. Chamomile is a powerful oil to use on the House of Growth because it promotes strength and courage and thus enhances our vocal expression with clarity and power.

The low, mat-like growth of chamomile keeps it close and firmly rooted to the Earth. It carries within its morphogenetic wisdom, a very strong grounding essence. The aroma of chamomile is fresh, sweet, and smells similar to freshly cut hay, and crisp apples harvested on a cool autumn day, with deep warm undertones of honey.

The grandfather of medicine, Hippocrates, once dedicated chamomile to the Sun, because it cured agues and fevers. The oil is distilled under an exacting formula, as are most essential oils, to retain the live molecules of the plant, or the soul essence, the fire of the plant. It must be distilled slowly, taking almost 12 hours for the proper distillation and with an equally precise temperature maintenance, the oil produced will be a deep rich blue oil, with an abundant supply of azulen, a well-known anti-inflammatory ingredient. Chamomile is soothing, relaxing, and is a perfect sedative for those under stress.

Chamomile is another very spiritual oil that aligns with truth and creates an aura of protection around us. Chamomile is an excellent oil to be used in blends created for psychic protection, particularly when used in combination with lavender and frankincense. It brings the gift of courage to our being, helping us to feel safe in the world.

The trinity of talented oils is completed with the essential oil of melissa, Melissa officinalis, sometimes known as lemon balm. Melissa is a hardy, herbaceous perennial found native to Southern Europe. The essential oil is distilled from the leaves and the tops of the plants, and has clean, crisp, and warm, lemony notes to its aroma. Melissa is a quiet sedative by nature, and has a very profound calming effect on the speech, thereby empowering the alignment between expression and the Divine.

As far back as the 1600's we find the herbalist Culpepper

praising the ability of melissa to uplift spirits. Melissa is a very special oil and tends to be very expensive in pure form. When we consider the fact that it takes 7 tons of the plant to produce 2 1/4 pounds of the oil, we begin to appreciate the cost of this valuable ally. The term sacred would most certainly apply to the oil of melissa. Melissa has often been called "the oil that heals" due to its healing properties. Melissa has wonderful antidepressant properties, and by relaxing the throat center, allows for a relaxed manner of speaking, by removing nervousness from the system.

Melissa is indeed a welcome companion to all essential oils, and is always greeted with pleasure in this House. Relax, put your feet up for a spell, inhale deeply of the aromas of our guests, the essential oils, feast upon the glorious foods that serve to regulate the House of Growth, look upon the glorious soothing colors of the stones placed to enhance the healing of this center, listen to the sweet chants and notes that resonate throughout the House, and allow the truth to be expressed.

All of these ancient allies aid and assist in empowering our truth, and the graceful and honest communication that can result from the consistent anointing with consecrated oils specifically blended to heal and balance the House of Growth, our temple of communication.

Anointing the House of Growth

On the night of the full or new moon, light the candles of the altar and spend a few moments in meditation asking for guidance and assistance from the angels and masters to assist in creating the finest anointing chrism for the House of Growth. We might want to anoint ourselves before beginning to mix the oils with a little frankincense to induce a more meditative and intuitive state, anointing our third eye and the palms of our hands, perhaps the solar plexus or 3rd House, and the soles of our feet.

We would then begin to blend the chosen essential oils into our anointing chrism. We would start with the essential oil of lavender. Again, using a one ounce bottle with dropper top or orifice reducer cap, we would begin by pouring the lavender into the bottle, following with chamomile, and finishing with angelica. Follow our prescribed dosage of essential oils from the previous chapters using the oils most beneficial for this blend. Once we begin to become very familiar with the oils, their properties and their potency, we can begin to intuitively blend with varying amounts of oils, using caution to ensure the oils are not too strong or completely undiluted when using on the skin to avoid any possibility of toxicity.

Lavender and blue chamomile are oils that can be used neat on the skin as they have very potent anti-inflammatory properties and are very healing for the skin, so this blend can be stronger than the general prescribed dosage of 28 drops. There are some oils that we would never use neat on the skin, as they are exceptionally caustic, such as cinnamon, clove, thyme and various other oils. Hence the formula of 28 drops pure essential oil to one-ounce carrier oil. With that said, we can always use more essential oils to make the blend more potent, but use caution as essential oils are very powerful and can be toxic in extremely high doses. When first beginning to use essential oils, it is best to err on the side of caution, and follow the prescribed formula of 28 drops of essential oil to one ounce of carrier oil.

The more we use anointing as a tool to develop our intuition, for meditation and in our daily practice, the more intuitive we become and eventually, the oils will begin to communicate and command very exacting formulas for anointing chrisms. It is suggested however, to begin with the basic formula of 28 drops of pure essential oils per one-ounce bottle.

Another consideration for using the prescribed formula when mixing oils, is to remember that essential oils are precious commodities and should never be over-used or squandered in any application. Also bear in mind as we begin to become more acquainted with the world of essential oils, we begin to realize that essential oils and the plants from which they are derived are becoming more and more precious, some even becoming endangered or extinct.

More plants and trees are becoming endangered species due to overharvesting and improper stewardship. If we are to preserve this precious sacred resource, we must become conscious stewards of the land, and conscious consumers of the products produced from the harvesting of the plant world. We are losing species everyday in the rush to harvest and procure, so we as consumers must begin to practice conscious consumption of all precious resources. The biggest protection we can offer this resource is to become educated about where our oils are distilled, how they are harvested, whether or not they are sustainably grown, etc. When this happens we not only ensure the future availability of essential oils, but we become conscious stewards of our Earth.

Once we have poured the right amount of essential oils into the bottle, fill the remainder of the bottle with our chosen carrier oil, organic jojoba oil being the oil of choice, or if the blend is to be used within 4-5 months, we can use pure, organic olive oil. Take the bottle and mix the oils, invoking the consecration of the oils into an anointing chrism (see previous chapters).

We would then place the anointing chrism into the light of the full moon (if blending on a full moon, if blending on a new moon, we can still set it outside overnight to absorb the light of the stars and other planetary influences.

When it is time to anoint the House of Growth, take the anointing chrism and dispense 5-8 drops of the anointing oils into the palm of the hand, and then begin to rub the chrism onto the throat area, working from the sternum all the way up to the jaw, and then all along the jawbone. Gently massage the oils into the entire area, invoking the color of turquoise blue into that area. Then gently hold the hands around the throat, being cautious to use light pressure, as the throat area is extremely sensitive to pressure from touch. Hold the area for a few minutes allowing the oils to penetrate into the bloodstream and work their magic there, softening, balancing and healing this entire area.

There will be a relaxing and softening that occurs in this area, and the one being anointed might feel impulsed to make sound, laughter, crying, screaming, chanting, all manner of sound might be elicited when anointing this area. Just know that a release and a healing are occurring and allow for that to occur, holding the area until the sound no longer wants to be made.

Take the turquoise or chrysacolla gemstone and lay it across the throat, or create a circle of stones around the throat area resembling a gemstone necklace, allowing the energy of the crystals to infuse the oils with their electromagnetic frequency.

We would then use our tuning forks, the forks of C and E, or the forks of C and G here. Again, we can direct the sound into the House of Growth, or we can move the sound through the air above the House, all the way around to the ears (cautioning again to keep the forks far enough away from the ear to avoid a vibrational resonance that might be too intense) When first learning to use tuning forks, it is advisable to begin practicing on our own bodies and ears, so that we become very familiar with the feel and sound of the vibration, and the distance needed to keep the ears safe. Always err on the side of caution when working with tuning forks around the ears, as holding the forks to close to the ears can cause damage.

If chanting the bija mantra of Ham, we could chant the mantra at the same time as using the tuning forks or instead of, chanting with the intention of bringing the sound into the throat and vibrating it into the throat of the one being anointed, or if we are anointing ourselves, just allow the sound to resonate throughout this House. We would chant Ham in a six beat rhythm. We can also chant the sound of EH into this House as well, and continue to vibrate that sound throughout the entire throat area.

Spend a few minutes working with the sounds and allow the sound vibration to carry throughout the House. There is a whole study of science devoted to the power of sound and the affect that sound has on the body, and it is another powerful modality to enhance the affects of the anointing.

When we have finished anointing this House, we can either lie still in front of the altar noticing the effects on the throat center or 5th chakra, or we can move onto the House of Intelligence, or the third eye, the sixth chakra, and home to our intuition and visionary clairvoyance.

Chapter 8

The House of Intelligence
Temple of Intuition

Intuition is our contact between

conscious and subconscious.

We do whatever comes spontaneously to us,

then suddenly, we are aware of thought.

Intuition is really the key to thinking.

Buckminster Fuller

Intuition
The power or faculty of attaining
direct knowledge or awareness
without rational thought or inference.

Webster's Collegiate Dictionary

Intuition is the magical power that charges the House of Intelligence. The 6th House, or temple of intuition is the birthplace of Christ Consciousness, and it is with the development of intuition that we enable our ability to recognize and partake of the spiritual reverie that occurs in the House of Spirit. The House of Intelligence, or 6th House, has been referred to also as the "third eye" and is a place of deep wisdom and awareness. The yogic name for this energy center is ajna chakra.

In the ancient Egyptian times, this House was called the Eye of Horus and was cultivated as a fine garden of wisdom, coaxed and encouraged to flower and bloom, opening consciousness to all the ancient sacred mysteries. Schools were developed to train disciples through practices designed to awaken intuition and spiritual wisdom. The Ancient Mystery Schools have flourished, albeit through some civilizations in secrecy, and still continue to this day, awakening people to their inherent Divine powers.

The House of Intelligence is located in the center of the forehead, between the brows, and extends in and around the base of the skull, including the first cervical vertebra.

The temple of intuition radiates a brilliant sapphire blue color, with blue rays of light dancing through the House instilling telepathic energy and bringing light to the face of ancient wisdom.

The House of Intelligence is sourced from the direction of the west on the medicine wheel. The season of autumn flows through this House, and it is a time when life energy begins its retreat into sleep, or deepens to a quiet still place within. This center is the place that gathers the setting sun, and is the place where ego death begins to make room for the rebirth into the Divine.

Quite often, as this House begins to come into balance and alignment, there is a dance that occurs between the will, or ego, and the guidance of our Divine nature. This dance sometimes leads us into what has been termed "the dark night of the soul," or the death of the ego, and can be a somewhat painful time in which there is a great deal of emotional suffering.

It is generated by the ego's strong survival instinct and the battle it undergoes when the Divine will wants to move to the forefront of control. During the dark night of the soul, we are forced to look at areas within our selves that need healing, and oftentimes when looking at areas that need healing, we must first identify the hurt, which means diving into the experience of that hurt. Therein lies the suffering and the resistance to wanting to do our "inner work". But until we identify and work to process the hurt out of our body, it continues to manifest in ways that often no longer serve us, such as anger, mistrust, fear of abandonment etc.

Once the work is complete, and you awaken to a new sense of reality, it is often accompanied by an ability to see things through the eye of wisdom, or the third eye, the eye of the Mystic.

When we begin to awaken to the power of Spirit or the Divine, we are impulsed in the House of Heart with feeling, which then commences to make its presence through understanding and knowledge in the 6th House. When this happens we will oftentimes be moved to devote our selves to deep meditation and contemplation. It is within the practice of meditation and prayer we become able to link with the vestigial third eye, the pineal gland, which actually has the capacity to perceive light. The French philosopher Rene Descartes called the pineal gland, "the seat of the soul" and it is here in this House that we are able to glimpse and cultivate our understanding of Spirit as a soul within our bodies.

When we spend time enhancing and fortifying this House, we begin to develop our power of vision and sensitivity, which enables us to step into the vast library of ancient wisdom. This is not the wisdom of mental learning, but the much deeper, more prolific wisdom of eternity, which we begin to intuit from deep within our soul. It is through this vestigial third eye that we are able to intuit and understand the deep ancient wisdom that resides in the center of our soul, found in the 4th House of Heart.

The color deep indigo blue will enhance and stimulate this House. By invoking the angels of color, we can beckon assistance with the infusion of color.

Invocation to the Indigo Blue Ray

**I call upon the Elohim of the Indigo Blue Ray,
To pour your magnificent royal blue color
Into, and around my sixth House of Intelligence.
Awaken, activate and empower
My intuition and vision
With your deep, royal blue ray.
deep sapphire indigo ray,
Spill your radiance through all of my being,
And bring me to my Divine truth.**

The supreme choice of foods prepared to nourish and enhance the balance of this House will include the blue violet food group. Eggplant, plums, grapes, purple cabbage, turnips, artichokes, and purple flowers such as violas and violets will nourish the glands and organs that reside in the 6th House, the pineal, the pituitary, the brain, eyes, ears, and nose.

Sound Therapy

When using audio therapy to balance and activate this House, focus on the tones of EE (as in free). By consciously directing these tones through this House, we can create a resonance of activation. The notes of a high A, also have an extremely stimulating effect on the House of Intelligence. We would use the tuning forks of C and A, or a combination of C, A and C. When purchasing tuning forks, you will receive both high and low C in your set, and both of these can be used to help calm the central nervous system, or to stimulate this House. The combination of C and E can also be used here as well, which seems to really stimulate the visionary capabilities of this House.

The bija mantra used for the House of Growth is the mantra of OM in a six beat rhythm.

The master and mistress of this House, when aligned and balanced, are deeply connected to their inner guidance, share peace of mind with their insight fully activated, and are masters of the self. They will be very balanced in world affairs, and while in complete union in relationship, will not exhibit behavior that is co-dependent, but rather come to relationship with a desire to move more into intimate Communion, allowing relationship to grow more into an expression of Divinity and conscious co-creation.

When this House is out of balance, we will find the master and mistress quite undisciplined, with a fear of success, or fear of failure, and a tendency towards hypersensitivity, and quite often unable to distinguish between the ego and the higher self, or Spirit. An imbalance here would also support manipulation, an enhanced ego, and will lead to eye problems, headaches and allergies.

In addition to color and foods that help to balance the House of Intelligence, there are many stones that will help to bring this House into alignment.

Crystals and Gemstones

O thou afflicted, tossed with tempest and not comforted, behold, I will lay thy stones with fair colors, And lay the foundations with sapphires.

Isaiah 54:11-12

The English translation of the biblical word, sappur, is sapphire and means "the substance of God's throne." It was said that in Medieval Europe the sapphire could induce powers of prophecy due to its stimulating effects on the 6th House and the pituitary and pineal glands. The sapphire will help to balance the pituitary gland, which is thought to be the power center of imagination. It is though imaging, that our creations are born, whether it is the visualization of a healthy body, or the creation of a splendid symphony, it is within the Temple of Intuition that all of our creations are envisioned.

The sapphire assists in maintaining alertness, enabling a clear and brilliant vision. The sapphire also helps to disperse sadness, due to its inherent spiritual frequency. Sapphire was recommended in Medieval Europe as a charm against plague, sorcery, headache and eye troubles.

Sapphire invokes the celestial light of the blue ray, which is quite naturally a protective, healing and soothing color, and so induces peace, wisdom and clairvoyance into this venerable House. While sapphires can be prohibitively expensive for the use of stone layouts on the body, another distant relative in the sapphire blue family, and much more affordable, is lapis lazuli.

Lapis lazuli is another esteemed guest in this House, and since the beginning of recorded history has long been associated with royalty. The Egyptian Kings and Queens were always adorned with lapis, and wore crowns of gold and lapis, representing the merger of royalty with the Divine light of gold. It was believed that lapis lazuli was a power stone capable of penetrating the subconscious, and allowing a clear communication with the Divine.

Lapis was revered for its ability to surrender our minds into the guidance of our higher self, our Divine Presence. The blue ray works with lapis to establish a layer of protective energy around us, preventing psychic attack, or the infusion of negative energy into our auric field or etheric body.

Lapis was sacred to the Goddess Isis, and she was known to have worn lapis to initiate wisdom within, a signature of the all-seeing Eye of Horus.

The beautiful blue lapis will help us to move out of depression and into the House of higher wisdom, the temple of Intuition, The House of Intelligence.

Essential Oils

Myrrh, Commiphora myrrha, was one of the three gifts brought to the baby Jesus by the Three Wise Men, and has been prized throughout the history of civilization. It has been used for incense, religious ceremony, perfume, embalming and a myriad of medicinal cures by many of our ancestors.

The essential oil is distilled from the resin collected from the stem and shoots of the myrrh tree. Myrrh grows wild and is cultivated in North Africa, Northern India, and the Middle East. The exotic fragrance of the oil is deep, Earthy, warm, and spicy with woody notes peppered through the aroma.

Myrrh is an excellent oil to use in skin care preparations due to its soothing, anti-inflammatory, antiseptic and astringent properties. Myrrh is also an excellent oil to use for healing respiratory conditions.

The fragrance of myrrh has long been prized for its ability to awaken spiritual awareness. Myrrh has the gift of stilling the mind, calming fears and raising our states of consciousness. Myrrh raises the frequency of Spirit, making it permeate our awareness, allowing the Divine wisdom to activate our visual perception and intuition.

Sailing in on a light summer wind, sandalwood, Santalum album, makes its lofty entrance into the House of Intelligence to bring wisps of Spirit into the temple of intuition. Sandalwood oil is distilled from the heartwood and roots of the tree, which is commercially grown in India, Indonesia and as of recently, Australia. Every tree is numbered and registered by the government, and it is not until the tree has matured at 40-50 years that the essential oil is harvested. The indiscriminate felling of the entire tree up until fairly recently as led to the species becoming endangered, and as a result also, the oil is now harvested in a similar manner as maple syrup.

As of this writing it is no longer possible to procure pure sandalwood, Santalum album from India, as it has been over harvested. The best sandalwood now comes from Indonesia, with an upcoming presence from the Australian growers. This is another example of the improper stewardship of the plant world and the resultant disappearance of Indian sandalwood, which has been the finest in the world.

Which means that as consumers we must be ever so diligent in educating ourselves about the source of our products, how they are made, grown, and harvested in order to keep the supply of oils available in the future. Unfortunately, the indiscriminate consumption of oils has led to a good many plant sources for essential oils becoming endangered. It is our responsibility as consumers to know where every product, essential oil, (or whatever we purchase) comes from, how it's grown, (organically, or with pesticides), made, and the manufacturing ethics of the company marketing the product. By becoming better educated as consumers, we can help to prevent more plant and animal species from becoming endangered or even worse, going extinct. As stewards of the planet it is our responsibility to become aware and take preventative, educated action.

Sandalwood oil is still one of the main oils used in Ayurvedic medicine and is of particular note in skin care due to its anti-inflammatory properties. It has also been a main ingredient in some of the more exotic perfumes.

Sandalwood has been found to help dispel negative programming in the cells and is one of the most useful oils to use when looking to clear subconscious and genetic programs from the cellular system. Sandalwood helps to increase oxygen around the pituitary and pineal glands, thus inspiring the production of melatonin and serotonin, the hormones responsible for inducing spiritual and meditative states, which assists with our complete surrender into the Divine.

Sandalwood was used in the process of mummification and for embalming, helping to preserve the bodies of Kings, Queens, and the Pharaohs. Sandalwood has also been burned as an offering to the Gods and Goddesses throughout history.

Sandalwood is a sacred treasure, and it will resonate throughout the House of Intelligence, dancing with the light of Spirit.

Another beloved friend to the House of Intelligence is the highly prized oil of frankincense, Boswellia carteri. Frankincense is another of the more sacred oils, and was also one of the gifts brought to the baby Jesus. The rich, exotic, spicy and woody essential oil is distilled from the resin "tears" extracted by scoring the bark of the small tree that grows only in the Middle East.

Highly valued for its spiritual properties, frankincense has been used throughout time in religious and spiritual ceremony, and has been used by the Catholic Church to invoke the Spirit of Christ.

Frankincense is the only known anti-tumoral oil and is also helpful in the treatment of skin disorders and is extremely valuable for the healing of respiratory conditions, due to its analgesic and anti-inflammatory properties.

Upon inhalation, frankincense relaxes us, allowing for a transcendent move into a deeply spiritual state of awareness. It has long been used to induce such states in religious and spiritual ceremony. Frankincense carries within its soul, an ancient wisdom that enables us to awaken vision and intuition within.

Frankincense has been called a "gift from the Gods and Goddesses," and restores our birthright, the connection to higher states of awareness. Frankincense has been known throughout the entire world as an anointing oil, and it is mentioned in the Bible more than 50 times. Due to its incredible oxygenating properties, frankincense also stimulates the release of melatonin and serotonin from the pituitary and pineal glands, thus enabling a move into bliss and altered states of Divine awareness.

Anointing the House of Intelligence

Note the phase of the moon and choose either the new moon, or the full moon for the ceremony of creating the sacred blend of essential oils for the chrism to be used during the anointing rite.

Light the candles on the altar, place fresh flowers on the altar as an offering of thanks for the mystical presence of the Divine during the course of the blending of the sacred anointing chrism, and for the actual ceremony of anointing the House of Intelligence. The altar could be covered in a cobalt blue cloth to bring the vibration of that color to the ceremony and to help balance the 6th chakra, the House of Intelligence. It would be a good idea to anoint ourselves with oils, and to spend some time in meditation and prayer, connecting into our intuition so that as we create our anointing blends, it is with a higher state of awareness and consciousness. We can also ask at that time to have the presence and pleasure of the angelic hosts, masters, teachers and guides that work with us, walk with us and protect us to be present and aid and assist in consecrating the anointing blend so that the essence of Divine presence is infused into the oils.

Take the essential oils of frankincense, sandalwood and myrrh and place them on the altar until it is time to use them in the blending of the anointing oils for the 6th House. Take our one ounce bottle, and proceed to pour a desired amount of sandalwood essential oil into the bottle, followed by a desired amount of frankincense oil, and then lastly a small amount of myrrh. Myrrh is a very pungent oil and can quite overpower the other oils, and hence the reason for a small amount of it being used in the anointing blend.

Once the essential oils have been poured into the bottle, we would then fill the remainder of the bottle with organic jojoba oil and cap the bottle. Again, take the chrism between the palms of the hands and briskly rub the blend back and forth between the two palms until all of the oils are completely blended together. You will know when this has happened as there will be no separation of the oils visible to the eye.

We can then take the oil and hold it between our palms and close the eyes, ask the Holy of the Holies to come and infuse the anointing chrism with the power and significance of the Divine and ask that the oils become sacred and consecrated, so that whomever is anointed with that chrism is also made or declared sacred and holy.

Allow the energy of the Divine to pour into the blend, vibrating it into the highest possible frequency of the Light. Feel the light moving through the oils and raising the frequency into a state of Love.

When ready to anoint the House of Intelligence, set up a massage table in front of the altar, or lay down upon a soft cloth laid in front of the altar. Take the anointing chrism from the altar and drop 3-5 drops into the palm of the hand. Place the cap back on the chrism and return it to the altar, and then dip a finger into the oils in the palm and begin to rub the oils onto the forehead in the area of the brow, all the way up to the hairline, focusing in the area between the brows and slightly higher. The oils can be rubbed across the forehead and onto the temples and lightly massaged in.

Once the oils have been dispersed, gently lay the hand across the anointed forehead and hold the hand there, invoking indigo blue light into the hand and the oils, and eventually into the forehead and third eye. It is helpful to see the third eye area spinning like a wheel, opening and activating that energy center. Allow the hand to remain there for a few moments so that the oils can penetrate the skin and be fully absorbed into the bloodstream, where the activation is at its greatest.

We would then take a small lapis or sapphire gemstone and place it over the House of Intelligence and allow the healing, balancing and activating properties of the crystal to work its magic.

Then take the tuning forks of C and E, or the other combination of tuning forks, and gently rap them against the soft part of the patella and allow the sound of the forks to circle 4-6 inches away from the ears, and then aim the ends directly at the 6th House. Allow the sound to move through the House of Intelligence activating that energy center to allow for a gentle opening. Many people have reported seeing visions when having the House of Intelligence anointed, and particularly with the frankincense which has the ability to awaken those higher states of visionary awareness.

We would then chant or tone the sound of EE or the bija mantra of OM and direct that sound into the House of Intelligence. If we are anointing ourselves, focus on sending the sound into that area of the forehead, and if anointing someone else, gently bend the head close to their forehead while chanting and channel the sound directly into the forehead.

Allow the sound to continue to move through the House and let it mix with the essential oils where it can combine to create an even deeper experience of awakening within the House of Intelligence.

If just anointing this House, keep the eyes closed, and let the inner wisdom and vision continue to be enriched by the holy anointing and move into meditation and silent prayer. The anointing of this House will often induce powerful visions, and an opportunity for our meditation to bring great insight, and it's therefore recommended to spend time in meditation after all anointing work.

If we were going to continue to anoint the rest of the body, we would then move onto the House of Spirit, or our 7th chakra.

Chapter 9

The House of Spirit

Temple of Wisdom

We are not human beings

On a spiritual journey

We are spiritual beings

On a human journey.

Teilhard de Chardin

Unction

The act of anointing as a rite of consecration or healing.

Webster's Collegiate

Long heralded as holy, our crown chakra, the uppermost seventh energy center of the body is the House of Spirit or the temple of wisdom, and is home to our understanding and the reception of spiritual wisdom. This House is the location for the intellect, but more importantly, this is the House where our spiritual wisdom is disseminated by the intellect and accessed for knowledge. It is in this House where our greatest evolution occurs, where our Spirit becomes illuminated with the Divine incandescence that continually pours forth from the Heavens. It enters the House of Spirit, the crown chakra and pours down through the entire House, radiating through each and every cell of our bodies.

It is here in the House of Spirit that we become conscious or aware of our selves as Divine. It is within the House of Spirit that the major recognition of our spiritual evolution occurs, the "awakening of consciousness." This is the part of our consciousness that is concerned with perceptions of separation and unity with the Divine.

In yogic traditions the House of Spirit is called the Sahasrara, and is depicted as a lotus flower with 972 petals, and is often called the thousand petaled lotus. This House is the place where all Universal energy and truths are filtered into the body and disseminated as information that the body and mind can understand and integrate.

This is the House where we make the conscious choice to move away from unconscious behavior into more enlightened states of awareness and action.

**The major shift in human evolution is
from behaving like an animal struggling to survive,
to behaving like an animal choosing to evolve.**

Dr. Jonas Salk

Inside the House of Spirit we are given a choice within our spiritual evolution, the choice between living our lives staying present, conscious and aware of our true spiritual natures, or to live life struggling with suffering as we remain unconscious, oftentimes lost in the drama of our lives. It is within the House of

Spirit that the choice is revealed and decided. Do we let the Divine into the driver's seat, or do we allow our egos, so often deceived by greed, anger and fear, continue to run us?

The truth is that the thinking part of our intellect, the mind, never really has total control over our lives. The ego, our personality, loves to think it controls everything that we think, say and do, but the real truth is that our soul runs the show from behind the scenes, only allowing the ego to think there is some modicum of control in life. But the truth is, the Divine is ultimately the one behind the wheel. Therein lies an amazing discovery, as we learn how to release control completely and allow the Divine will of our souls to direct our course, and stay conscious of that fact, we help to alleviate our struggles, and the inherent suffering we so often create for ourselves.

The hearth of this royal palace burns brightly with the amethystine purple color of the Violet Ray of Illumination. The color purple has always been respected as a color of great significance and was often reserved for royalty.

Color can be made manifest to burn ever more brightly by invoking the color purple into this home.

Invocation to the Amethystine Violet Ray

I call upon the Master of the Amethystine Violet Ray,
Bring illumination to my House of Spirit.
Burn your violet flame
Through the veils of all separation
And reunite me with the Divine.

Another way to work color into this House is to hang leaded cut crystals in the window and as the sunlight catches the crystals, wonderful prisms of color will be projected into the room. As the sun hits the crystal, rainbows of color are projected outward, and it is possible to take the color into the eyes and transfer it to the appropriate House or part of the body needing a particular color through definitive intention. This technique works well for all the colors of the various Houses. When looking at the rainbow of colors that is produced by the crystals being penetrated with sunlight, we are able to isolate the desired color and take in the color and direct into our bodies or those we wish to bathe in color (taking care not to look at the color or absorb the color for longer than 30 seconds). We can absorb the color into our bodies and then project it to someone we are working on, again, intention playing the key factor in the transference of energy and color.

Cosmic energy lives here in the 7th House, side by side with the process of intelligence and thought. When residing in this House we are continually being sourced from the Heavens and it is with the wisdom of the Universe that we are able to anchor more of the Divine within the body, and more succinctly, into the temple of wisdom.

Clairvoyance and exalted states of joy are cultivated within this House, and dedication to Spirit is fed and nurtured here as well. Often visions are received or filtered through the 7th House and then given form with the third eye, found in the 6th House. We often intuitively sense our connection to the spiritual world through our crown chakra, or the House of Spirit, while the feeling nature of our awareness happens within the House of Heart.

The foods that are most nourishing for this House are plums, beets, purple grapes, blackberries, Marion berries, raspberries, mame, and passion fruit. There is another school of thought that suggests fasting as an alternative method of bringing balance to the House of Spirit by allowing the body to rest from the digestive process, which thereby frees up more energy to devote to meditative and energetic healing.

There are many glands and organs that are at home in this House. This House is the location of the pituitary gland, the pineal gland, the central nervous system, the cerebral cortex, and the brain.

There are many types of yogic practices that serve to stimulate this energy center, such as pranayama and certain asana postures that involve inverting the body. Yogis have practiced standing on their heads since the beginning of time so that as they allow the blood to flow into the brain, the pineal gland is stimulated, and there is a resulting release of the hormone serotonin, which is the hormone that is responsible for the state of bliss and altered states of awareness. This release of serotonin is accomplished so that at the end of our asana practice we can easily slip into the state of meditation. The ancient yogis believed that one of the primary purposes of asana practice was to ready one for the state of meditation.

The release of serotonin has been referred to historically as the release of amrita, which is a Sanskrit word meaning "without death". It is repeatedly referred to as the drink of the gods, and is said to grant immortality. This amrita, or ambrosia drips nectar into the body, and it's said that once we have dripped all of the amrita into our bodies and released that sac of ambrosia, we can then expire and make our transition out of the body.

Sound Therapy

When applying sound therapy, either through tuning forks or vocalizing sound or chanting, the tone UU (as in you) vibrates most effectively in this House. High B seems to balance this House particularly well, and assists with an elevation into Divine frequency, "whispering to the soft words of the Divine." Any of the tuning forks may be used to stimulate this House, but often the combination of high and low C with A work particularly well to open the crown.

The bija mantra used to work with this House is the mantra of Nada Brahma chanted in a seven beat rhythm. Nada Brahma is thought to be the sound of the Universe, or the voice of God.

In ancient times there were mystery schools where initiates came to explore the mysteries of life. These schools flourished in Egypt, Tibet, and Persia and were believed to have their roots in the ancient land of Atlantis.

Those initiates and seekers were taught to develop their psychic and spiritual powers through various techniques, exercises, and initiations. One of the most important initiations was called the Great Initiation Rite and involved chanting specific chants or sounds. They believed that the chanting would stimulate the pituitary and pineal glands with the vibration of the chant and allow the crown chakra and the third eye to open to higher states of awareness.

The initiates also believed that the opening of the crown chakra allowed higher vibrations of the Universe to enter into the auric field and into the body, which would allow for the body to become more balanced and move into healing. They believed that the neo cortex of the brain would be stimulated and that there would be a resultant release of endorphins into the body and bring a sense of relaxation and peace to the body. The stimulation of the pineal and pituitary also allowed for the release of hormones into the body and affected the entire endocrine system in a very beneficial way. The ancients have always known about the power of sound to aid and assist in the conscious evolution of one towards an enlightened state.

The House of Spirit holds the promise of faith and is represented in Native American medicine wheel traditions by the direction of above, or Great Spirit. It was thought that if one listened to the stillness, the Great Spirit from above could whisper the secrets. There is an unswerving faith that must be present to assist us as we enter into silence through meditation to enable us to hear the secrets of the Great Mystery.

Faith is an attribute which must be cultivated if we want to withstand the tragedies of human experience. Our faith is never greatly challenged when life runs smoothly; it's when the hurdles and stumbling blocks trip us up that our true faith must be called into action. Our deeply cultivated connection to the Divine is the cushion that allows our faith to carry us through the dark hours, knowing that we are only moving through a challenging time, and that challenge will again at some point in time fade, and we will be back on calm seas again.

The nature of our faith changes on its evolution toward maturity. We get tested in life, with pain and suffering throughout our lives, but as we mature and experience more of life's rocky roads and continually seek to practice some level of devotion to a spiritual practice, we become better accustomed to dealing with the issues with more grace and ease. This allows for a readiness to move through the experience more quickly, cultivating stronger and stronger faith with every experience. If we continually stay connected to the Divine thread that runs through everything, we become more and more adept at dealing with life's crises.

St. Paul explained faith once as the substance of things hoped for, but not seen. The Spirit of the Divine that exists in each of us relies on faith to keep us connected, alive, happy, and radiant. The true definition of faith is a trust or belief in a particular truth, or the more formal usage reserved for concepts of religion pertaining to belief in a transcendent reality or the Supreme.

When the 7th House of Spirit is shut down, one might exhibit the following emotional symptoms; no concern for others, feelings of superiority, joylessness, a lack of knowing one's true purpose, a disconnection with Spirit, and a lack of contact with reality. The physical symptoms of an imbalance in the House of Spirit might manifest as depression, schizophrenia, mental disorders, senility, dizziness, and even Parkinson's.

Someone who's 7th House is open and balanced would demonstrate a reverence for all of life, a behavior of self-less service to others, an ability to see the path that leads to benefit of the greater good, and a general mood of idealism and optimism about life. Outward signs of a happy, cultivated spiritual community are present in one's life, there is a connection with the dharmic mission in one's life, and they exhibit the ability to stay balanced in their spirituality while functioning well with their humanity.

Crystals and Gemstones

The human body is made up of electronic vibrations. Each organ and organism has its electronic unit of vibration necessary for the sustenance of, and equilibrium in that particular organism. A low electrical charge may be set up by the vibratory impulse of certain gems and minerals that can be transferred to the body, causing it to extract more of the particular elements in digested foods.
Edgar Cayce New York Times, 1910

Edgar Cayce knew of the ability crystals and gemstones have to affect healing on the body, as did our ancient ancestors.

One of the most powerful influences on the House of Spirit is the amethyst crystal with its deep hues of violet. Throughout the ages, amethyst has been heralded as a great healer in the mineral realms. Even today, the element which gives amethyst its royal purple color has yet to be discovered, some think it is due to the content of ferric iron, but perhaps it could be due to the fact that amethyst is a transducer of the violet ray, and has long been used in the healing and activation of Spirit.

Edgar Cayce said about the amethyst, "The vibration of this crystal can actually cause molecular change." Crystals have been used since the introduction of radios to transmit the electromagnetic radio waves, and for that reason it's easy to see how amethyst could conduct healing electromagnetic energy and have an affect on the body's molecular vibration.

This could be the reason that many say amethyst aligns itself with Mercury, the planet of higher communication. (We all remember Mercury, the messenger of the Gods and Goddesses).

Amethyst teaches us about humility, and supports the surrender of the ego to Spirit, or the more evolved part of our being.

Amethyst helps to clarify and purify our thoughts, and works to align and balance the thyroid gland, the pituitary gland, and the pineal gland. Amethyst will help to fortify and empower our ability to express love. It has been written about in the Egyptian Book of the Dead, dating its use back to 4,000 BC, about the time when anointing flourished in the temples of Egypt.

Amethyst helps to clear and quiet the random, mundane thoughts of the mind and allows for a deep surrender into medita-tion and is therefore an excellent stone to use when meditating, or to use on the altar to instill meditative energy into the sacred space surrounding our altars. Amethyst is a fabulous healing stone when used on the body, and we might conclude that the immersion into a meditative state could easily be the reason for our physical bodies responding to the presence of amethyst, and moving into a harmonized and balanced state of wellness.

Essential Oils

**He found her as she slept in the beauty of her palace.
She awakened at the fragrance of the god, which smelled
in the presence of his majesty. When he came before her,
she rejoiced in his beauty. His love passed into her limbs
which the fragrance of the god flooded.**
From an inscription on the chamber wall of an Egyptian pyramid.

There is no other fragrance that can be more powerful or can induce such rapture as that of essential oils, and one of the most sacred and holy is the ancient oil of spikenard, Nardostachys jatamanasi. Spikenard is an essential oil distilled from the dried and crushed rhizome and roots of the plant that is native to the mountainous regions of Tibet, Northern India, China and Japan. The oil is mainly distilled in Europe and the United States. The most prized oil of all comes from the Himalayas in the region of Tibet, and is very scarce and equally expensive.

Spikenard is in the family of Valerianancaeae, the family of valerian root, which is the source of Valium a well-known relaxant. It is a hypnotic essential oil, and induces a deep meditative state, which stimulates the release of serotonin and melatonin. It has tremendous anti-inflammatory, antibacterial, antifungal, and antiviral properties. Not only has it been used for medicinal purposes, but more importantly as an oil to take one into altered states of awareness in ceremony and religious rites.

There is no other oil more highly regarded by the Bible than spikenard, and it is mentioned throughout the chapters and verses. Spikenard was the oil Mary used to anoint the feet of Jesus before the Last Supper:

Then took Mary a pound of ointment of spikenard,
very costly, and anointed the feet of Jesus,
and then wiped his feet with her hair:
and the House was filled with the odour of the ointment.
St. John, 12:3

The Romans also used spikenard in the preparation of their more celebrated perfume, or the unguent called nardium, which was one of the most well known scented oils used at that time. Discorides also spoke of spikenard and attributed the oil with healing properties for indigestion, inflammation, and nausea.

Spikenard has the ability to elicit extreme states of altered consciousness, inviting us to dance into the light of Spirit. The warm, heavy, sweet and woody fragrance of spikenard is very similar to valerian oil, and has a somewhat similar aroma to that of recently harvested hay.

Spikenard is a fragrance long used for its ability to consecrate one as sacred, and to induce hypnotic, meditative states. It is an oil that helps us to transcend the limits of time, and enables an ability to live in a more sacred and holy manner.

Neroli, Citrus aurantium bigaradia, is another formidable presence in the majestic kingdom of essential oils. Neroli is distilled from the freshly picked blossoms of the orange tree. The blossoms sit at the uppermost reaches of the tree and are the part of the tree that grows closest to the sun. The fragrant, syrupy sweet flowers produce an essential oil that is true in its aroma to the source of its origins as a flower. Neroli is a rather costly oil, but considering the fact it takes 1 ton of flowers to produce 2 pounds of essential oil, we can certainly understand what makes this oil so precious.

There is nothing that compares with walking through an orange orchard on a warm spring afternoon with the heady, bewitching aroma of the orange blossoms enveloping you. The fragrance is so sweet, so strong, and so overpowering that soon all senses melt into the fragrance and you find yourself adrift on a fragrant cloud into the heart of Shangri-La. It is an experience that overtakes all of the senses and one cannot help but be moved by the fragrance.

Neroli is excellent for helping us connect to the illumination of the Sun, and the warmth of light, bringing joy, love and serenity to any disquieted soul. The essential oil of neroli is also a superb oil for dispersing depression, and is a very hypnotic sedative. Nervousness is dispelled instantaneously with the inhalation of neroli, and one just can't help but relax and smile when inhaling the powerful elixir of neroli. A clear, warm and happy House is the best welcome for Spirit, and neroli brings this essence to the House of Spirit. When you administer neroli to this House, the sensual aroma envelops us, and allows for merger with our Divine luminescence.

Another religious luminary in the kingdom of aromas is galbanum, Ferula galbaniflua. Galbanum is distilled from the resinous gum emitted by the cousin of our common perennial giant fennel plants. It is a native to Southern Europe, North Africa, and Western Asia and was said to have originated in Iran.

Its aroma is deep, warm, woody and very Earthy, and tends to inspire deep states of relaxation. Its rich aroma helps dispel anxiety and leaves us feeling refreshed.

Galbanum has been used for centuries for religious and spiritual ceremony. The Egyptians used it with myrrh in the embalming process, soaking the muslin used to wrap bodies in a combination of the two oils, due to its exceptional preservative properties.

In addition, galbanum contains antibacterial, antimicrobial, and antiseptic properties.

The Hebrews used galbanum for anointing as they recognized its ability to carry us into the Divine. Galbanum is a powerful oil to use for meditation, very hypnotic with its heady aroma, and works to initiate greater amounts of Divine wisdom into our conscious awareness.

Remember always, that these oils are only recommendations based on years of practice. As anointing is practiced more and more, the intuition will become developed such that our own guidance might direct us to use oils other than what are recommended here, and there is no end to the oils that could be used to help connect us to Spirit or the Divine. The only prerequisite is a distinct intention of connecting into our Divine inner awareness through mediation as we begin to choose and blend the essential oils

Each and every member of the plant kingdom seems to exhibit a sense of liveliness and Spirit. When we come to recognize the energy that propels us forward through life, also propels every other living species, we can begin to have reverence and respect for the plant world, and become better stewards of the Earth's resources. When that occurs, we will ensure the availability of these precious treasures.

Essential oils have walked beside us since the beginning of time, have healed us, carried us deeper into an awareness of Spirit, consecrated us as sacred and holy, and served to usher us through every passage in life, as well as heal any and all maladies that can befall the physical body.

Whether we choose to use one essential oil or many, each time we state the intention of consecrating our selves as sacred and Divine, the soul consciousness of essential oils support our connection with Spirit. Essential oils that have been consecrated as holy will in turn consecrate every thing they touch as holy.

There is no greater tool to help with our return to wellness, to wholeness and to the Divine than anointing. There is evidence that anointing has consecrated our walk since the beginning of time, and now as we are evolving in a world that continues to challenge us more and more, it is time for us to return to some of the more ancient techniques and tools that have assisted mankind from the beginning. Anointing aids and assists with our walk through life, enabling us to lead full, happy, and radiant lives, full of the knowledge that our true nature is that of Divine romantic beings, here to play the game of life and enjoy it to the fullest extent possible while we are here.

Anointing our selves on a daily basis with the intention of releasing the past, allows for all fear, which is built upon past experiences, to be released from our presence. By anchoring and experiencing our selves in every moment, we are fully allowed the opportunity to experience the Divine in all aspects of our lives.

In life, there are but two choices as to how we experience each moment: living in love, or living in fear. Living in love maintains that we only exist in the present moment, which is absolute truth. Living in fear represents an attachment to the past or the future, and almost always has nothing to do with the present moment.

By residing in the moment and truly living from love, we are no longer separated from our Spirit, and do not expend any life force looking to keep alive anything that is less than love. Living life in the state of Love is the grandest romance of our lives, and one that we can cultivate and keep alive with the practice of anointing.

Anointing the House of Spirit

Choose a date to create the anointing chrism for the House of Intelligence based upon the phase of the moon, either the full moon, or the new moon, depending upon the energy we are seeking to enhance when blending.

The energy of the new moon gives power to all new endeavors or projects that are initiated and so could be used to initiate new states of being or awareness. The full moon brings power to all levels of completion or harvesting, and we might want to choose a full moon when we are looking to heal an aspect of ourselves that is no longer necessary, or we want to harvest the fruits of our labors involving some long-term goal or project.

When creating the anointing chrism, take the prescribed oils of neroli, spikenard and galbanum and a one-ounce bottle and begin by pouring the neroli, followed by the spikenard and galbanum to the desired amount of 28 drops. Use the prescribed formula and instructions for creating the chrism from our previous chapters.

At the appointed hour, light the candles on the altar, place a fresh offering of flowers or a bowl of fresh fruit as an offering of thanks upon the altar, and set out the anointing chrism and tuning forks if they are to be used in the anointing ceremony.

If someone else is being anointed, we could set up a massage table or sacred cloth in front of the altar, and have him or her lay down upon the table or cloth in anticipation of the ceremony.

Take the consecrated anointing chrism created specifically for the House of Spirit, or the 7th chakra and pour 5-8 drops into the palm of the hand, replace the top on the bottle and place it back on the altar. Take a couple of fingers and dip into the sacred blend and apply to the crown of the head. Begin to gently massage the crown chakra, continuing to massage the entire amount of anointing chrism from the palm into the House of Spirit. Once all the oils have been massaged in, hold the palm over the crown and allow the oils to penetrate all the way into the skin, and then into the bloodstream where the chrism can begin to activate and balance the House of Spirit. Again, the one being anointed may very well feel the effects of the oils, emotion may come up or interesting visions, pictures or messages may come in. Allow a few minutes for the oils to absorb and then we can take the tuning forks and begin to work the sound into the crown chakra, empowering the oils with the sound vibrations.

We could also begin to chant the bija mantra of Nada Brahma while invoking the royal healing color of purple to descend down into the crown chakra, filling each and every cell with the healing and activating color. At the same time, we could also place amethyst crystals around the crown of the head.

Then we might chant the sound of UU, beginning the sound in the heart and carrying it all the way up into the head, vibrating the sound throughout the crown. If we are anointing someone else, we could hold our mouth close to their head and allow the sound to enter into and move through their House of Spirit.

Always when working with the House of Spirit, it is important that after we have activated and opened that chakra, we then seal it with light, so that there is protection for the crown as we move out into the world again. That can be accomplished by visualizing golden light coming out of the hands and running the hands over the crown sealing the entire head with golden light. It is also very powerful to ask our Guardian Angels for protection as well.

If we have anointed the entire body, we can run the hands and golden light down the entire length of the body, finishing at the feet.

Spend lots of time in meditation after the anointing, the one being anointed can feel very spaced out, and even possibly dizzy or weak. Until there is a complete grounding it is advisable to be reverent and respectful of the work, the oils and the sound vibrations, and allow the body to adjust to the new frequency before attempting to move back into the world.

It needs to be noted here that if you have anointed someone's entire body with oils, sound and energy, that there is a tremendous electromagnetic shift that occurs and will affect the molecular system of the body for some time following the session. There has been a dramatic shift in the cells and that shift will manifest for several weeks, and any number of symptoms might occur as a result. People can get dizzy, experience flu like symptoms, emotional outbursts, excessive elimination, all are common and not to be frightened by.

The anointing initiates a release of old patterns and beliefs that no longer serve us, and any of the above conditions are symptomatic of that release. The body and emotions will eventually get used to the new frequency and awareness, and any symptoms will subside. Again, a good daily spiritual practice or devotion helps immeasurably in anchoring the new energies and awareness fully into the body, mind, and spirit. It is very important after anointing all of the Houses, that one drinks as much water as possible for at least 3 days following the anointing, to flush anything that is released from the body.

It can not be said often enough that anointing is a very powerful tool to assist in the activation and awakening of Divine consciousness, and can be something that we practice on ourselves daily, or can be a ceremony created for a loved one where each and every House is anointed with the respective chrism prepared specifically for that chakra. Anointing on a regular basis assures the presence of the Divine within us, and aids and assists in keeping each House or energy center of the body completely balanced and aligned to ensure that we remain in a radiant, vibrant and healthy state. Anointing allows for us to move into higher states of awareness and helps to bring about a tremendous shift in our ability to see the Divine in all things, including ourselves, and it is in that enlightened state of awareness that each and every moment in our life becomes a miracle.

There are two ways to live:
you can live as if nothing is a miracle;
or you can live as if everything is a miracle.

Albert Einstein

Anointing on a regular and consistent basis enhances every breath we take, enriches every thought, word and action, so that we are constantly reminded of the miracle, in fact, with anointing, we can ***become*** the miracle!!

Chapter 10

The Seven Sacraments

and Corresponding Anointing Ceremonies

There is some kiss we want

with our whole lives,

the touch of Spirit on the body.

Jalaluddin Rumi

Sacrament

In Christian belief and practice, a sacrament is a rite,
instituted by Christ that mediates grace,
constituting a sacred mystery.
The root meaning of the Latin word
sacramentum is to make sacred.

Wikipedia

The most conventional definition of a sacrament means it is an outward sign instituted by Christ that bestows the recipient of the spiritual grace, blessings, and presence of the Christ. The Catholic Church believes there are seven sacraments or sacred mysteries and the Anglicans believe that the sacred mysteries are also based on the number of seven, which coincides with the seven Houses, the seven chakras, the seven pointed star, and the seven directions.

Eastern and Oriental Orthodox views ascertain that there are seven sacraments as well, but prefer to call them sacred mysteries, as they believe that it is impossible to name the something which is impossible to classify. Their belief is the Divine presence that impregnates every sacred rite and object is impossible to understand with the human intellect. Again, the presence of faith is called into action, as we begin to learn that the Divine presence of the Christ, God, Allah, Buddha, Great Spirit, or whatever term we use to define the indefinable, is something that we know with our hearts, not our minds, and it is within the heart we find our faith and our direct link to the Divine part of ourselves.

The seven sacraments practiced within the Catholic Church today consist of Baptism, Confirmation, Communion or the Eucharist, Renunciation and Penance (commonly referred to as Confession), Anointing of the Sick and Last Rites, Ordination, and Matrimony. Some of the sacraments are performed only once in a lifetime, others can be performed as often as one likes.

Some of the sacraments involve anointing with holy chrism, and others do not. The very fact that anointing is included in some of the sacraments attests to the power of anointing within religious ceremony practiced today within the Church. From experience, anointing can be a sacrament given at any time to activate the grace and strength of the Divine, and does not necessarily need to be given by an ordained priest of the Church.

The Catholic Church teaches that the effect of a sacrament comes by the very fact of being administered, regardless of the personal holiness of the person administering the sacrament, or ceremony. The Church also states that the sacraments presuppose faith and, in addition, through their words, and ritual elements, nourish, strengthen and give expression to faith. The sacrament of Baptism frees one from original sin and all personal sin, and makes the baptized person share in the glory of sanctifying grace. It imparts the theological virtues, faith, hope and charity and the gifts of the Holy Spirit, and marks the baptized person with a spiritual seal or character that indicates permanent belonging to Christ. In case of necessity, anyone intending to do what the Church does, even if that person is not a Christian, can baptize.

Compendium of the Catechism
of the Catholic Church, 224, 1213-1284

In other words, the laws of the Church don't limit ***anyone*** from performing a ceremony of Baptism; the only thing that is necessary is ***invoking the presence of the Christ***.

It is the intention we put into the ceremony that means everything. By invoking the presence of the Divine, we become clothed with the sacred grace of the Christ and as such, in a fashion, we become the messenger of the Divine and ordained to administer.

The following is a brief description of the sacrament, or ceremony of Baptism, and an example of a Baptismal ceremony to honor a newborn, or newly indoctrinated member of the community. We will use an entirely different combination of essential oils for this ceremony, as an example of another grouping of oils that would be appropriate for anointing.

This ceremony or sacrament is an opportunity to assist individuals in their spiritual progress and growth in holiness.

Baptism

Baptism is a welcoming sacrament offered unto a new life entering into the family and/or the community. When a child is born and acknowledged by the family and community, there is a conscious declaration by the tribe to accept responsibility for the physical, emotional, and mental care of the child, and to inspire and cultivate faith within that child.

Baptism is also a way of celebrating and enacting the awareness of God in a child, or a new member of the family.

Baptismal ceremonies are also a commitment to teach the child or newcomer about their spiritual heritage according to the belief systems that operate within that specific tribe, community, family, culture, and or, Church.

The ceremony of anointing for Baptism consecrates our commitment to the Divine soul of the newly born, and assists in the grounding of said to its Earthly walk. It is within this context we see the association of Baptism to the first House, the House of Essence, or the root chakra.

Baptism can occur at any point in one's life, but should be particularly considered at the time of any great birth, the birth of a child, the birth of a new love, or the birth of a new creation, etc. The sacrament or ceremony of Baptism can accelerate the flow of Divine Love, Grace, and Spirit, into one's life.

Imagine a child conceived of a passionate, spiritual union between a man and a woman, a child created in a shared moment of ecstatic union between two beloveds. Would not this child know somewhere within the sub-conscious the momentum of that union, the divine energy of Love that propelled the child's soul into physical form?

Baptism is the acknowledgment of a soul as holy, born of love, the highest frequency known to the human, and an expression of the Divine. With the acknowledgment of one as a holy vessel of love, Divine Spirit, or God, we are recognizing the inherent attributes of that soul as omniscient, omnipotent, and omnipresent, as are stated in the Bible, the attributes ascribed to God. This should always be the focal point and main intention behind a ceremony honoring a birth, and the entrance into a family and community. In a religious sense, Baptism welcomes the newborn into the community of the Church.

The Baptism also represents liberation from sin within the religious communities, and when performed within the confines of the Church, a Baptismal ceremony will include some level of banishment of sin and extraneous spirits as to free the individual of anything that does not serve the entry into the kingdom of Christ, and the entry into a Divine lifestyle.

According to the Church, Baptism is always followed by a ceremony of Confirmation, confirming the walk into a religious or spiritual life. In some religious traditions, the Confirmation ceremony will directly follow the Baptism, and in other traditions will come when a child has matured into early teen years. The sacrament of Confirmation is the spiritual seal that is placed upon the confirmand that signifies a child of God and in some Catholic Churches involves the anointing with frankincense. The ceremony of Confirmation will also include the Eucharist or Communion, which is the taking of the blood and body of Christ.

Anointing following a Baptism

If you do not already have an altar created in your home, you will want to create one for the ceremony. Always prepare a place of significance for the Baptismal ceremony to occur, creating an altar is an excellent way to establish an aura of reverence and a sacred space with which the Baptism and subsequent Confirmation and Communion ceremonies can occur. One might also want to include some item representing the birth as well.

The color of red seems to resonate the highest with this ceremony, and could be represented by red flowers, crystals or gemstones, candles or even a red altar cloth. In the middle of the altar should rest the vessel of anointing oils specifically created for the ceremony, as well as a vessel of water, which is traditionally used in most Baptismal ceremonies.

It is essential to the ceremony of Baptism to include some sort of water rite, preparing either a sacred bath with oils and flower petals, or a bowl to dip one's hand into with oils and petals. The religious significance of water represents washing away original sin, but can also be interpreted as a means in which to immerse one's self in the holy waters. This water should be also be blessed and consecrated to hold the vibration of the Divine. Baptism is a bath of water into which the imperishable Word of God, or the consecration of said water is enlivened to produce its life and faith giving effects.

**The word is brought to the material element,
and it becomes a sacrament.**

*St. Augustine - on Baptism
Catechism Section 2 1228*

Again, we see the power of our words and our intention in bringing forth consecration to any material object. In preparing for the Baptismal ceremony, we would want first to create the setting, a sanctified altar, the holy water with which we will baptize and the anointing chrism that will confirm the one being blessed. The ceremony of Confirmation will also include a laying on of hands which has been done traditionally within the Church, which will impart to the newly baptized the gift of Spirit and completes the grace of Baptism. The rite or sacrament of Communion, which could follow the Baptism and Confirmatory anointing, will involve some level of ingesting the body and blood of Christ or a facsimile of that ceremony and represents taking in fully the Spirit of Christ, or the Divine Presence.

The three sacraments of Baptism, Confirmation and Communion become a holy trinity that will allow for a redemption of all sins and confirmation of said confirmand into the community of faithful believers who will support the child or adult on its path of faith, grace, belief and the practice of spiritual or religious virtues. The Baptism signifies the beginning of new life, Confirmation is the strengthening, and Communion, nourishes the disciple with the body and blood of Christ to transform the disciple in Christ.

To bless the water fill a lovely bowl with fresh water, one could also use a tub if the entire body is to be immersed as part of the ceremony. Baptism in water can also happen in the outdoors in a sacred pool, or river, followed with the confirmatory anointing with a sacred chrism.

Pour a few drops of the essential oils of frankincense and balsam fir into the water, and float flowers, or place crystals into the water to energize the water. Then have all who are attending, place their hands over the water and infuse a blessing of their choice into the water. Ask that the water be consecrated by the Divine, Holy Spirit, God, Angels, Masters, Brahman, Great Mystery, Allah, or whoever it is that we source ourselves with. The more traditional religious blessing is a prayer of epiclesis, or prayer of consecration, which would be something that would seek the power of the Holy Spirit to be sent upon the water, so that those baptized in it may be born of water and the Spirit. It is also important that all attending enter into a state of prayer or meditation, being directed to invoke the presence of the Divine into the ceremony for the one who is to be baptized.

After the prayers of invocation, the one being baptized will have the water poured over their forehead, or immersed into the water three times. The significance of three is a triple infusion representing the immersion into God, Christ and the Holy Spirit, and also represents purification, justification and sanctification.

The community that witnesses and plays part in the ceremony of Baptism are very important as it is the community of believers that support the newly baptized on the path to faith, and it takes a community of faithful to cultivate belief within the newcomer. The blessing concludes the ceremony of Baptism and the anointing of Confirmation with a consecrated chrism can follow to confirm the newly baptized.

Anointing for Confirmation following a Baptism

The ceremony of Confirmation is traditionally performed once in one's life and it generally follows the sacrament of Baptism. It is called Chrismation (In the Eastern Churches: Anointing with holy myron or chrism) because the essential rite of the sacrament is anointing with chrism (an oil mixed with balsam). It is called Confirmation because it confirms and strengthens Baptismal grace. The ceremony of Communion can be practiced at anytime throughout one's life. It is a sacrament or sacred gift that may be given any time one wants to deepen and empower the awareness of Spirit.

With this anointing, the confirmand receives the "mark" or a holy seal of the Holy Spirit, or Divine Presence, and ensures the belonging to Christ and the promise of Divine protection in the ultimate destiny of humanity.

A Confirmation chrism, or myron, for an infant must be *greatly* diluted, as their skin is extremely sensitive. Essential oils partic-ularly suited for the ceremony of Baptism are lavender, balsam fir, and frankincense. The properties of lavender are revealed in chapter 7, the properties of Frankincense in chapter 9.

Balsam fir, abies balsamea, is an evergreen tree that grows to heights of 65 feet or more and has been used by Native Americans for sacred ceremony for years. Fir is a member of the Coniferae family and grows in frigid and temperate climates around the globe. They are some of the tallest and oldest growing trees on the planet, and have an enormous ability to weather dire temperatures, which gives the essential oil powerful properties.

The oil is distilled from the trunk, leaves and branches, and contains a multitude of healing properties, which are said to be warming and reviving to the nervous system and the respiratory system. The fragrance of fir is known the world over and is most associated with Christmas trees, a clean, woody, fragrant aroma, similar to pine.

One might even be led to believe that the strengthening and fortifying properties of the essential oil would be the reason it was chosen to be used for Confirmatory chrism, or anointing myron.

When blending the anointing chrism for a Confirmation ceremony, the dilution for infants should be one drop of essential oil per four teaspoons of carrier oil. For adults the dilution changes to 28 drops of essential oils per one ounce of carrier oil. For immediate use only, (due to its fragile shelf life), pure, organic olive oil would be the choice carrier oil, due to the many biblical references, which attest to the inherent value of olive oil.

Begin by pouring the appropriate amount of balsam fir first, (depending on whether or not you are blending for an adult or child) allowing fir to be the predominant oil in the blend. Follow with the addition of lavender and then frankincense oils, and then finish with the carrier oil filling up the rest of your bottle. Consecrate the chrism, which is described in detail in the previous chapters. The consecration of the sacred chrism is an important action that will precede the ceremony, and begins with a renewal of the baptismal promises and seals the mark of the Divine onto the said confirmand. A religious example of a consecrating prayer might look like this:

The liturgy of Antioch expresses the epiclesis for the consecration of the sacred chrism (myron) in this way: Father, send your Holy Spirit upon us and on this oil which is before us and consecrate it so that it may be for all who

are anointed and marked with it holy myron, priestly myron, royal myron, anointing with gladness, clothing with light, a cloak of salvation, a spiritual gift, the sanctification of souls and bodies, imperishable happiness, the indelible seal, a buckler of faith, and a fearsome helmet against all the works of the adversary.

Catholic Catechism Section 2 1297

While this could be an example of an invocation, and quite religious in nature, it serves only as an example of an invocation to consecrate the anointing chrism. Another example of an invocation which might be more generic and used for more spiritual ceremonies and belief systems, could be something like this:

I call forth the angels, masters, teachers and guides that dwell in the highest realm of love and light to come forth and pour your love and your light into this chrism so that it is blessed with the Divine Presence of the Christ and all who are anointed with it will feel the power and presence of the Divine. Allow all who are anointed with this chrism to be sealed and marked with the light of the Divine, infusing them with grace, love and protection.

Once the invocation has been called forth and poured into the anointing chrism, the chrism could then be placed in a significant area on the altar to gather more energy from the sacred objects located upon the altar until it is time to be used in the ceremony.

During the entire ceremony of Confirmation have everyone present hold an energy or thought of gratitude for the presence of the Divine in all things. Focus upon the presence of the Divine within the newborn child, welcoming the newborn child into the community, and accepting responsibility for the nurturing of them. Not only is the ceremony of Confirmation an opportunity to invoke the presence of the Divine, but also, even more importantly, it is a declaration of the inherent Divine nature in us all. It allows us all to become responsible for holding the energy for this soul to be protected, and consecrated throughout its entire journey on this Earth.

At a designated point any welcome prayers or words of dedication may be spoken and offered by those attending. This ceremony can vary, alter, or grow in any direction as is desired. It is not limited to any belief system in its creation, and can also be composed of different religious or spiritual rites. It is the intention of invoking the presence of the Divine as a blessing unto the newly born and the subsequent seal of the Divine that serves as a protective mark upon the newborn that carries the importance within the sacrament or ceremony of Confirmation.

The ceremony should proceed with the newly born being anointed with the chrism, retrieved from the altar. A few drops of the holy anointing oils should be poured into the anointer's hand and then, dipping a finger into the sacred blend, anoint the forehead, the soles of the feet, the palms of the hands, the spine, and the heart of the newly born. The following prayer is traditionally spoken at the same time the anointing occurs to confer the power of the Divine: "Accipe signaculum doni Spiritus Sancti" (Be sealed with the gift of the Holy Spirit). The consecration of one as Holy and Divine is always the principal focus within the sacrament of Confirmation.

There are some within the religious structures who believe that Baptism, Communion, and Confirmation should go hand in hand, and have even been referred to as the Holy Trinity. Experience shows that anointing seems to be much more powerful when performed in a succession of three, perhaps indicating a distinct correlation.

Anointing for Confirmation of a Young Adult

Confirmation, sometimes referred to as Chrismation, is a universal ceremony consecrating a code of honor and grace into one's life and actions. The definition of Chrismation is a confirmatory sacrament in which a baptized member is anointed with chrism, and generally follows the ceremony of Baptism, either immediately after or shortly thereafter. Confirmation can also happen as a young member of the community begins to move through puberty, and should also precede a deeper immersion into a more intimate reunion with a Christian or spiritual lifestyle.

Every society and faith recognizes a coming of age, or a time when a younger member of the tribe is ready to stand alone as an adult in the world. There are ceremonies performed throughout many cultures around the world honoring this rite of passage. The ceremony of Confirmation is a sacrament that can also be performed at the time of puberty, and is quite often called a rite of passage, signifying leaving the childhood behind and entering into a more mature persona.

The rite of passage ceremony that occurs within Native American cultures can involve a young man going out on a vision quest at the time of puberty, to seek his soul and commune with Great Spirit. Puberty signifies a time in a young woman or man's life when they embark upon the path into adulthood. The ceremony of joining the moon lodge would be part of the rite of passage performed on a young woman coming of age as she begins to enter her moon cycle.

The ceremony of Confirmation is traditionally performed once in one's life and it generally follows the sacrament of Baptism. It is called Confirmation because it confirms and strengthens Baptismal grace. The ceremony of Communion can be practiced at anytime throughout one's life. It is a sacrament or sacred gift that may be given any time one wants to deepen and empower the awareness of Spirit.

This coming of age is a time of one's coming to power, and is closely tied with the second House of Essence, the home of our emotional body, and the place where we establish our relationship to our self. As parents or guardians, we can hope to inspire a spiritual walk for a young adult by acknowledging them and empowering them with an anointing ceremony, created to assist in consecrating them as Divine Spirit.

The rite of Confirmation represents a journey of discovery, empowering self-esteem, integrity and embracing a code of honesty within our lives. By consecrating our selves as sacred with holy anointing oils, we insure the presence and pleasure of the Divine, and the subsequent empowerment inspired by that presence. The anointing with a consecrated chrism seals the mark of the Divine upon anyone receiving the blessing.

When creating a rite of passage for a young adult such as a Confirmation ceremony, it is important that the young adult be involved in the creation of the altar. It is an acknowledgment of this soul's passage into adulthood. Again, objects or pictures of spiritual or religious significance to the one being honored should be placed upon the altar. Specific items that are representative of childhood, or symbolize adulthood would be an important addition to the altar. The color mandarin orange is a very powerful compliment to this particular sacrament or ceremony and could be represented by flowers, fruit, or an orange altar cloth.

The most powerful anointing oils for this anointing ceremony of Confirmation are as mentioned in the section above. The most important part of any ceremony or sacrament of Confirmation will be the intention behind be the creation of anointing oils and their transformation into chrism.

The level of your intention and power of invocation to the Divine will dictate the infusion of spiritual or religious blessings into the anointing compound.

When the ceremony is to ready to occur, have all gather in front of the altar in council, and ask the young adult to sit in the center of the circle. Ask that each member of the tribe take a moment to share something about that person, maybe their observations of that person and who they see them becoming, and to give a blessing or prayer for the ceremony. They might also want to offer wisdom that could be of benefit to the young adult on their path.

It would be very beneficial to have the young person sit for some time in meditation as preparation for the ceremony, and to begin to immerse completely into the deeply spiritual presence that will permeate the ceremony.

After everyone has had a turn to speak, allow the young adult to speak whatever it is that they want to offer. Then we could ask the young one to lay down in the circle, and have everyone there lay a hand on the person, invoking the presence of the Holy Spirit to be infused into the young person, and to be consecrated and sealed with the mark of the Divine.

The one offering the anointing would then take the anointing chrism and pour a few drops into the palm of the hand. Replace the cap onto the bottle, and then place a finger into the oils and spread them across the brow of the young adult, the heart center, and the palms of the hands and the soles of the feet. All the while invoking the presence of the Divine to come into and declare the young adult sacred and Divine. Ask everyone there to hold that intention and allow the energy to move throughout the young one.

If anyone has a chant or prayer to offer, allow him or her to speak it to the young person, or everyone could just sit quietly in meditation to honor the consecration of the Divinely anointed one.

Confirmation of the soul as Divine Presence is an affirmation and sacred seal that protects the confirmand and dedicates one to the service of the Divine. This rite of passage celebrates the confirmed re-connection to the Divine. Confirmation could also be an indication of the establishment of one's own set of rules or code of honor.

The final sacrament or ceremony of this sacred trilogy is Communion.

Communion

The sacrament of Communion has also been called the Eucharist, a word derived from Greek meaning thankfulness, gratitude, giving of thanks.

Today the name Eucharist is still used by the Catholics, The Eastern and Oriental Orthodox, the Anglicans, United Methodists, and Lutherans. Most other Protestants prefer Communion, or the Breaking of Bread.

The sacrament of Communion was born out of the Last Supper, and is performed as a rite or act of worship that nearly all Christians perform in order to fulfill what they believe to be the instructions that Jesus gave to his disciples during the Last Supper. On the night of his last meal, Jesus broke bread and according to Paul the Apostle said, "This is my body which is for you, do this in remembrance of me." And in the same manner with the cup after supper said, "This cup is the new covenant in my blood. Do this, as often as you drink it, in remembrance of me". Thus was born the Eucharist or the sacrament of Communion, and can serve as a reminder whenever we break bread or begin a meal to give thanks for the meal and the life-giving properties of the food and drink that nourishes our body and feeds our soul.

If we are to interpret the words of Jesus, anytime we break bread and consume with the intention of remembering Jesus, we take him into us, the same holding true of the sacred cup, drinking him into us. Offering grace before a meal is based on the tradition of giving thanks for all the blessings in our lives. A ceremony of Communion can also be a celebratory feast to give thanks for the new member of the tribe.

This sacrament most closely resonates with the 3rd House of Transcendence, as it is the location of our power center, as well as the location of our stomachs.

So almost any anointing ceremony that we would create to emulate the sacrament of Communion, we would want to include some offering of fresh bread to symbolize the taking of the body of Christ into us, and the drinking of consecrated wine or grape juice to symbolize the imbibing of the blood of Christ.

These symbolic gestures represent taking the light of the Divine fully into our bodies and amplifying our own inner light of Christ. The bread and wine should also be consecrated before consuming to insure the presence of the Divine.

The very name of Communion could be indicative of the reconnection to the Divine that occurs when practicing a ceremony of anointing, Come-u-n-I-ONE is asking for a reconnection to the ONE, the Divine to occur, and is the fundamental reason we would create a ceremony of Communion. Anytime we are looking to re-confirm our connection to the Source, the Divine, or to the Christ, we can create a ceremony of anointing.

In early Christian times, there was a ritual feast known as the agape feast, which was always held on a Sunday, and eventually became known as the day of the Lord, and is the basis for Sunday becoming the day that most religions claim as the Sabbath and most auspicious for religious ceremony. Agape is a word that means love, and these love feasts were celebrated more as a means of celebrating Divine love than human love.

So anytime we want to have a ceremony of Communion, after the anointing, we could prepare and serve an agape feast and include the breaking of bread. This could be the basis for partaking of the bread, or we could simplify the ceremony by placing fresh bread upon the altar that could then be broken up and consumed as a part of the rite.

The Church believes that only an ordained priest or bishop is capable of consecrating the Eucharist for the sacrament of Communion, however, they also state that others, who are not priests may act as extraordinary ministers of Holy Communion and can distribute the sacrament to others.

One could easily interpret that to mean, if we ordain ourselves, or declare ourselves sacred and holy through the process of consecration with a sacred anointing chrism, we are then capable of offering Communion as a sacrament to others. We are certainly not looking to usurp the Church and its priestly powers, it's more an act of emulation, and the offering of the sacraments with our anointing ceremonies is a call to remembrance of the Divine.

Again, when we ask to be consecrated by the Divine, when we invoke and open ourselves to the presence of the Divine, it manifests within us and we become that.

Sacrament of Marriage - Sacred Partnership

Therefore, I come forth to meet thee,
diligently to seek thy face, and I have found thee.
I have decked my bed with coverings of tapestry,
with carved works, with fine linen of Egypt.
I have perfumed my bed with myrrh, aloes, and cinnamon.
Come, let us take our full of love until morning,
let us solace our selves with love.

Proverbs 7

One of the primary characteristics of a sacred partnership, even more important than the love shared between two beloveds, is the sacred relationship we entertain with our selves. The symbolic interpretation of the sacrament of marriage encompasses the loving commitment we make to our selves, to love, honor, and respect every aspect, including the shadow side, of our beings until the end of our human path. We cannot begin to establish a truly healthy, loving relationship with another, until we are deeply committed to forgiving and loving every part of our selves.

When we begin to listen to the messages from our heart, we know that taking care of our selves becomes a necessary spiritual task, and it is not an act of selfishness, but an act centered in the self. When we anoint our hearts with the sacred chrism blended for this holy sacrament, we are consecrating our commitment to loving the self to the deepest depth within our hearts. We are consecrating the love of the positive and negative aspects of our selves, merging the polarity of our masculine and feminine principles, allowing for union within us, and **kindling the Divine spark** that has ignited passion for thousands of years.

The consecrated unified heart of love awakens a passion for living, loving, and sharing our hearts with the world. It is in the centered heart of love where a deep spiritual union with a beloved becomes possible.

The other aspect of sacred partnership is the love shared between two beloveds. It is an honor to be blessed with a sacred partner, to touch, kiss, hold, and love the Divine in human form. It is the closest we can come to loving Spirit in form. Relationship allows us the window of opportunity to learn the true expression of who we really are.

Such partnership brings along with it the gift of transcendence. By allowing us a much deeper glimpse into our personality, we are encouraged to burn through fear, limitation, and unhealthy behavioral patterns, thus promoting a deeper level of loving, and the ability to transcend negative aspects of the ego. The gift of marriage in a sacred partnership allows for that transcendence to occur at a grand level. The true gift of partnership is growth and evolution of our souls, for marriage by its very nature allows us a deep look at where we hold love back, and allows for us to heal wounds that keep us from exploring the deep levels of intimacy that marriage wants to bring.

Relationship will challenge us like nothing else. It will challenge us to look deep within our selves to see exactly what parts of our nature still need to be healed. Our partners can become our greatest teachers about the self, and why our beloveds should be honored, respected and always held in unconditional love, no matter how angry or upset we may become. Learning to love unconditionally is one of the true gifts of a relationship.

The sacrament of marriage, the anointing of a beloved union (be-love-d, unIone), most readily partners with the fourth House of Heart, the center of the body energy system where love is most easily and abundantly found. Anointing is a sacrament given to assure that the union within our selves, and the union between two beloveds becomes a sacred partnership. Anointing becomes insurance that the Divine operates inside each individual, as well as within the partnership.

Partnership becomes essential when seeking complete union of the Divine. Partnership allows us to learn more about our selves in a way that we never could alone. When we are without a partner, there isn't the perspective necessary to discover where our ego still holds fear, worry, obsession, etc. Partners are wonderful for showing us where in our personality we still need to grow, what issues we need to work with, and where we hold love back.

Relationship can be the gateway to true healing and deep intimacy if we are bold and brave enough to plunge in with all of our hearts and souls.

Relationships often bring a fusion of complementary opposites or reintegration of polarities, (male-female, yin and yang, etc.) leading to a gradual rediscovery of primordial unity. This transcendence of opposites is a transcendence of the entire cosmos, because this shift abolishes duality, there is no more separation.

The embrace of the masculine and the feminine creates a unification that emanates throughout all physical, emotional, and psycho-mental aspects of the cosmos into unity, the One, or the Divine.

Sacred partnership allows the beloveds a continual process of self-discovery, discovery of another, and discovery of the Divine at the same time. The three processes are completely integrated with one another.

An inherent aspect of a sacred partnership is the recognition of the libido, manifested as sexual drive but not to be considered as only sensuality, rather as the soul's ardent yearning for spiritual, or Divine union.

There lies within each of us an abysmal thirst and insatiable hunger to reach union with the Divine, perfected through the union of opposites. Union allows the dynamic, positively charged (yang) energy of the male to merge with the passive, magnetic, receptive, and negatively charged (yin) of the female, creating an extreme intensity of energy. This intense level of energy impulses the Heavens and the Supreme reveals itself to us in an indescribable union with the Divine.

Anointing for Sacred Partnership

An altar should be created to honor the gift of love. Anything that represents love can be incorporated into the creation, pictures of a beloved, spiritual masters or teachers, and objects of loving memory such as an item received from a loved one. The colors of pink or red have long been associated with love. Fresh roses have also been considered the symbol for eternal love and make a beautiful addition to an altar created to honor love. Pink or red candles are representative of the color of love, and when lit, represent the eternal flame of love. We may also wish to write down loving prayers, messages, or endearments of love to be placed upon the altar. A picture of the beloveds should hold a place of honor on the altar, a symbol of the ceremony consecrating the partnership.

When creating an anointing blend for this sacred blessing, the oils of rose (see chapter 6), bergamot, myrrh (see chapter 8), and jasmine are particularly empowering.

Bergamot, Citrus aurantium bergamia, was named after the Italian city of Bergamot and is where the oil was first sold. Bergamot is native to tropical Asia, but is now cultivated in Italy, California, and the Ivory Coast. The tree is much smaller than the orange tree, and typically only grows to 15 feet. Bergamot has been used since the 16th century in France, and has been mentioned in many old manuscripts and herbals. The oil is a light-colored greenish-yellow color with a sweet, fruity fragrance and base notes of balsam.

Bergamot, along with neroli, is considered by some to be one of the best essential oils when treating depression. The oil is obtained by cold expression of the peel of nearly ripe fruit, and used neat on the body, can make the skin somewhat photosensitive. It has many actions, including analgesic, antiseptic, anti-smasmodic, and can aid and assist in digestive disorders, as well as being a parasiticide. It is a powerful oil to uplift the heart, and combines particularly well with rose and jasmine.

Jasmine, Jasminium officinale is a genus of plants of some three hundred species, some evergreen and some deciduous, most of whom have a sweet, hypnotic white flower. The plant originated in India, China, and Persia, and in fact, the name jasmine is derived from the Persian word yasmin.

Jasmine is one of the most important plants in the perfume industry, and the annual world production of jasmine is from 12-15 tons.

Jasmine is one of the most hypnotic and intoxicating of all the floral oils and has been used for years for its aphrodisiac proper-ties and hence our inclusion of it in this blend.

The anointing blend should be held and the invocations of Divine love be called upon to consecrate the oils. The anointing chrism should then be placed within the heart of the altar while any songs, prayers, or declarations of love are professed. When the time comes to anoint yourself, and or, a beloved, the crown of the head, the brow, the throat, the heart, and the palms of the hands are indicated. Anointing with essential oils on a regular basis, re-commits us to our own self-love and to that of loving another.

The true commitment of sacred partnership must always begin with a devotion to empowering our own self-love. The love of another grows out of this union with our Divine selves.

Anointing to consecrate a marriage is a powerful way to invoke the presence of the Divine into a ceremony honoring the partnering of two beloveds. The anointing chrism can be blended as above, and would be used to anoint both beloveds, one at a time, following their vows to one another, and before they are declared husband and wife. The minister or officiate performing the ceremony would anoint both beloveds before pronouncing the husband and wife or at any other time when the partnership is to be consecrated. It could also be part of the marriage ceremony to have the beloveds anoint one another as part of their vows.

Ordination

Ordination
The ceremony of ordaining.

To Ordain
To invest with ministerial or sacerdotal functions;
confer holy orders upon.

Webster's Collegiate

When we recognize the Divine is omnipotent, omnipresent, and omniscient, we come to the realization that as vessels or temples of the Divine, we are manifested with the same trinity of attributes. Each of us embodies the Divine, and as such, we are all powerful, all present, and in all things.

A ceremony of Ordination can be performed whenever we seek to elevate our selves into that state of remembrance. Each of us can be ordained as priest or priestess of the Divine. Not to take anything away from the very holy nature of the Church and the hierarchy of power that has been established to give structure to the Church, we *can* ordain ourselves, and our loved ones and confer the presence of the Divine as emissaries of Love and Divine

Light. Even though the Church or religious organizations may not recognize us as true priest or priestess, the essence of the Divine will nevertheless bless us with the holy and sacred presence when called to do so, and we do in fact become emissaries of the Divine, or priest and priestess.

The path to Ordination is a deeply spiritual and personal journey. It is a journey inspired deep within, or can often be instigated within the community as a call to Ordination or a position of eminence.

The sacrament of Ordination is directly related to the 6th House of Intelligence, the energy center where intuition, Divine wisdom and intelligence reside. As Spirit makes its journey upwards, empowering spiritual development in its wake, Ordination awakens a conscious opening toward the Divine.

The ceremony of Ordination, when performed with sacred anointing oils, stimulates the intuition and recognition of Divine wisdom. We are elevated by the presence of these sacred aromatics into supreme posts of eminence, and activated into recognition of our selves as Divine emissaries.

Anointing for Ordination

The setting for a ceremony of Ordination will vary greatly according to the specific dictate of said Ordination. If the Ordination is an event accorded to our selves, the setting can be small and intimate. If the Ordination is decreed by community as part of indoctrination to a post of eminence within the community, such as would the coronation of a king or queen; the setting would be more inclusive of an audience.

In either event, an altar should be created specifically honoring this great rite of passage. The altar can include all religious or spiritual objects significant to the one being ordained, and to the community, pictures of religious or spiritual masters, prayer cloths, candles, flowers, or any other significant items of relevance. Deep royal blue, a color known for its association with royalty is the color most beneficent for this ceremony.

The intention behind a ceremony of Ordination is to elevate one into a supreme post of eminence, a religious or spiritual post of the Divine.

The oils of choice for a ceremony of anointing would be

frankincense, myrrh and spikenard (see chapters 8 & 9). These holy oils lend themselves particularly well to consecration as they have all served for thousands of years as the more eminent spiritual and religious oils.

When we ordain our selves and others, we are recognizing the light of Divine love that emanates from each of us. We are also recognizing the wisdom and intelligence of the ages that resides within each of us. In addition, we are declaring our selves consecrated as king and queen, priest and priestess, or even God and Goddess, all male and female embodiments of the Divine and willing to live by a moral set of spiritual or religious virtues and inevitably, as a minister of those said devotions and virtues. There is no higher post into which we can elevate our selves than that of a conscious vessel of the Divine.

Ordination can also be performed anytime we slip into a place of forgetfulness, or at a time when we seek to elevate further into conscious realization.

The areas of the body most eager to be anointed during a ceremony of Ordination are the crown of the head, the brow or "third eye," the back of the neck, and the palms.

Confession, and the Retrieval of Spirit

We are coming to a near universal understanding that union with the Divine can't fully occur carrying the burdens of negativity, fear, or guilt. A practice of confession, or the release of negativity, fear, or guilt through admission, allows for a subsequent retrieval of Spirit. This confession is a call to the sacred Divine self to assist us in consciously recalling the full breadth of our Spirit back. The release of fear, guilt and negativity from the body allows for a richer expression of the Supreme.

This ceremony can be a challenging one as we seek to let go and forgive our selves for any dishonesty, corruption, fearfulness, or guilt due to negative actions and words. When we allow these emotions to dominate our reality, we block the reception of love. With an honest confession of such acts, we can begin to move into forgiveness within our selves for our thoughts, words and or actions, and subsequently, ask for forgiveness from anyone who has been affected by the acts or words.

As the loving energy of the 4th House travels upward into the expressive energy of the 5th House of Growth, it is here that the sacrament of confession most closely resonates. The 5th House is home to our expression and vocalization of truth.

The ceremony of confession and the subsequent retrieval of Spirit, commands a supreme act of willpower, because, in order to fully embrace the essence of Divine Love, we must first face our dark shadows and transmute them into light. Acknowledgment is often the first step in transformation or transmutation, but we must also feel the power of our shadow side, and then, accept and love that aspect of our selves. Through this process, we can come to know and embody the act of compassion and understanding in our selves and in turn, toward others.

The ceremony of soul retrieval is sanctified by the application of anointing oils as a process toward which the reward is, once again, union with the Divine. To confess our shadow side allows for the healing and forgiveness to begin, whereupon Spirit more fully aligns with us. It also enables us to become much more aware of our thoughts, feelings, and emotions, and the motivation for words and actions, which leads to a more conscious mode of thought, word, and action in life.

As with all anointing ceremonies, there is always an aspect of our selves that is cleared or cleaned from our body, mind, and emotions, so that whatever holds us back from embracing the Divine completely, is cleared and the Love can then subsequently fill us and bring about true forgiveness and healing.

One of the most powerful tools available for the consummation of body and Spirit can be the ceremony of confession and the release of negativity which then allows for a reconfirming of one as Divine. The greatest assistant in assuring an invocation and consequently, a consecration of the Divine, is the anointing with essential oils following any confessional ceremony, or emotional release.

Anointing for the Retreival of Spirit

We would want to perform the ceremony in front of the altar, which could be covered in cobalt blue cloth to accentuate the healing color for the 5th House.

The inclusion of some sort of burning rite can be a very powerful addition. Initially we want to release the energy and emotion of confession by burning our recorded thoughts and words on paper in a fire created for just that purpose. We might even prefer to send the thoughts and words to be released into the flame of a burning candle or fireplace, etc., and watch the power of the fire transmute them into light. It is hoped that the power of burning externally, can alleviate the need to burn internally, although, it is generally the burning that we do internally that leads us to some desire to release the pain and suffering and move into a subsequent healing. The process of burning, leads us to the emotion that needs to be addressed. As the poet Rumi once said, "I **want** burning. . ." Rumi knew that burning, or suffering, as in the path of the Buddhist tradition, brings us closer to Source. The burning or suffering causes us to put attention in areas within our personalities that create drama and conflict. To know peace, we must be free of drama and conflict, and it is there that we find our Source, the Divine.

There is another practice that could also be considered for inclusion in this ceremony. Often, a symbolic, or actual cutting (of cords, paper, or material designated specifically for this purpose) can assist in profound release. We might want to take the cords to be cut, and express the act or words that are being confessed into the cords, and then it would be appropriate, and perhaps impera-tive that the cords are then burned or cut, so that an actual release may occur. Equally important, we should acknowledge when the event is complete, and offer prayers of gratitude for being finished with the experience and the subsequent release of energy that occurs from the cutting or burning.

As we burn or cut through these emotions, we are left with a more open vessel, to House even greater levels of our Divine nature, the Spirit of Love. At this point, anointing with a chrism can now fully invoke the Divine to fill us.

The anointing oils most appropriate for the ceremony of confession and spiritual retrieval are rose, lavender, and angelica (see chapters 6 & 7). The chrism used during the ceremony of spiritual retrieval should be anointed on the crown, the throat, the shoulders and the back of the neck, at the occipital bone.

It bears repeating again, and probably could never be overstated, that intention must be the key ingredient in every ceremony, altar, chrism, rite, prayer or invocation. Know that through the ceremony of confession and the subsequent invocation of Spirit, that all is forgiven and released. As the 5th House is the House of expression, it is vitally important that the confession or release is vocalized or spoken, to fully release the emotion, words or experience from the system. Such release will allow for complete immersion in the Divine.

Last Rites, or the Provision for the Journey

Anointing of the sick is the ritual of anointing a sick person, and has also been described using the more archaic synonym "unction" in place of anointing, as unction of the sick.

In previous ages the sacrament was known by a variety of names, e.g. the holy oil, or unction, or the sick, the unction or blessing of consecrated oil, the unction of God, the office of the unction etc. In the Eastern Church, the later technical term was euchelaion, or prayer oil. When these words were written, the official name of the sacrament in the Latin Rite of the Roman Catholic Church was Extreme Unction (meaning, Final Anointing) a name attached to it when it was administered, as one of the "Last Rites", only to people in immediate danger of death, and in that instance is known sometimes as Viaticum, a word whose original meaning in Latin was *provision for the journey.*

Early twentieth-century Catholic Encyclopedia

Are any among you sick?
They should call for the elders of the Church
and have them pray over them,
anointing them with oil in the name of the Lord.
And their prayer offered in faith will heal the sick
and the Lord will make them well,
and if they have committed sins, these will be forgiven.

James 5:14-15

Throughout history essential oils have assisted with healing rituals and practices in cultures and traditions around the world. It has been hypothesized that the profound healing work of Jesus was assisted with the use of essential oils.

The sacrament of extreme unction, commonly referred to as "Last Rites," is a sacrament in which a critically ill or injured person is anointed and prayed upon for salvation. This sacrament has most traditionally been administered only once in religious traditions at the time of one's death. The definition of extreme unction: the act of anointing as a rite of consecration specifically to heal. But an even deeper level of understanding of extreme unction, hereafter referred to as salvation, could also indicate a necessity for the rite of anointing on a daily basis. In the sacrament of salvation, we desire to release the unnecessary physical and emotional baggage we've acquired through the course of our living. We can then move into an acceptance of that which we are leaving behind and allow for our entrance into a new realm of experience, and a new redemption with the Divine. This very process of anointing on a daily basis to release attachments to that which no longer serves us, can prepare us for the time when we leave our bodies and pass out of this life, through the death process or journey.

This sacrament offers us an opportunity to live fully present in each moment, and allows us to live in a state of gratitude for every moment we are alive. By anointing our selves on a daily basis with essential oils particularly consecrated as chrism for this ceremony of salvation, we release all that has passed from us on a daily basis, including events, emotions and even people. In the allowance of releasing all that has moved away from us, we come to live more fully in the present and we do not waste energy trying to keep the past alive.

As we live more fully in each moment, we become more and more present in our consciousness, and in the wisdom of that certainty, we experience our daily life as truly Divine.

Salvation is most closely linked to the 7th House, the home of Spirit, and **the** energy center of Divine inspiration. Throughout history there have been recorded healings of a critically ill or injured person that have come about in a most miraculous fashion, with the only explanation being the presence of the Divine. When we commit our selves to a daily practice of anointing we allow for the miracle to occur.

When it is time for someone to make their journey out of the body, anointing with consecrated essential oils blended specifically as a chrism for salvation can greatly soothe and assist in the detachment from this world and ease the transition into the next. (In the deaths that I have attended, I have watched the oils bring such a deep level of peace and relaxation to the process of expiration, and I know that anointing chrisms are a critical component of ease and grace, when we are faced with releasing this world, and making the journey into the next.)

Anointing for the Provision of the Journey

The creation of an altar provides an arena of reverence, love, and intention for the journey to the other side. All sacred and holy objects will magnify the power of intention set forth in the ceremony of salvation. Again, anything of spiritual importance or significance should be placed upon the altar, which could be draped in a rich amethystine purple to enhance and enrich the 7th House inviting Spirit fully into consciousness. The color purple also has deeply significant healing properties imbued within it. Having an altar created in the room where someone is getting ready to leave their bodies is a powerful way to surround that person with the Divine in the form of sacred objects, candles, flowers etc.

As is true with all ceremonies, this sacrament becomes as individual as the creator's belief systems. There is no correct or incorrect way to perform a ceremony. Paramount in importance is the intention set forth when consecrating oils into chrism and anointing one into union with the Divine. Prayers or offerings of gratitude are often symbols of our acceptance that the union or re-union with the Divine has occurred.

The anointing oils most appropriate for this particular ceremonial anointing chrism are frankincense, blue chamomile, lavender, and spikenard (see chapters 6, 7, & 8). The areas of the body most responsive to this specific chrism are the crown of the head, the heart, the palms, and the soles of the feet. It is very important when anointing someone who is leaving their body, to allow them to inhale of the oils deeply and often. The oils seem to bring a calming quality to the breath, the emotions, the mind, and to the very soul so that any fear of the journey can be dissolved and the person can gently exhale and softly dance into the light.

With an exhale of the breath the soul begins the journey out of the body, just as we begin our journey into a body as newborns with an inhale. The fragrance of the anointing chrism aids in slowing the breath and with each exhale there is a surrender into a deeper state of relaxation and release. Anointing the body with the chrism allows for the physical body to be sanctified and inspires a sweet release for the soul to make its journey into the light.

Soft angelic music will also be of great assist in the journey, or chanting the sound of OM. It is advisable to have candles burning in the room, so that there is a constant source of light to serve as a reminder of the journey ahead.

The ancient Sanskrit Mahamrityunjaya mantra is a wonderful mantra to recite to aid the soul in detaching from the body. Mantras are religious or mystical poems or syllables, typically from the Sanskrit language. Repetitive recitation of the mantra is used as a spiritual conduit to create a vibration that instills one pointed concentration. They have also been used for various religious ceremonies to accumulate wealth, protect health, detach from the body and various other purposes.

When saying a mantra, there is significant impact when reciting the mantra for a minimum of 108 times. A mala or sacred rosary can be used to count the number of repetitions. The mala is a beaded necklace with 108 beads traditionally used to count mantras. (The number 108 has profound spiritual implications. The number 1 signifies the One, or the Divine Source, God with which we are each an expression. The number 0 represents the empty state we need to move into in order to experience the One, and the number 8 represents the Infinite, or the endless expression of the One.)

The Mahamrityunjaya mantra is as follows:

**Om Tryambakam Yajamahe
Sugandhim Pushtivardhanam
Urvarukamiva Bandhanan
Mrityor Mukshiya Maamritat**

The literal translation of the mantra means:

**We Meditate on the Three-eyed reality
Which permeates and nourishes all like a fragrance.
May we be liberated from death for the sake of immortality,
Even as the cucumber is severed from bondage to the creeper.**

One could also chant the names of God, Jesus, Hail Mary, or recite the Lord's Prayer if there is more religious prerogative dictating the words, using a rosary to count the incantations.

It is helpful for the one making the journey out of the body to be surrounded with loved ones who have reconciled the event and hold the space for the one to make the journey home into the arms of Love, held in a sweet embrace by the beloveds who have known and loved them in this life. Prayers of forgiveness can be spoken by any and all who need to reconcile before the journey is complete, even as simple a prayer as:

I forgive you, please forgive me, let's forgive each other, let's forgive ourselves, please, thank you, Amen.

When any loved one is holding on to the one leaving, it can hold the person here, and make for a more challenging time in releasing, so all of that needs to be reconciled so as to allow for an easy surrender of the body.

Diffusing lavender essential oil into the room is an excellent way to instill deep relaxation to all who are in the room and to allow for a deep level of surrender into the journey of the transition.

Once the last breath has been let go, stay with the body, and hold onto the heart chakra singing and chanting until the heart center grows cold, as there is an assurance at that point that the soul has made its transition.

The ancient Greeks had a custom of anointing the limbs of the departed with perfumed oils as evidenced in Homer's Odyssey,

But when the flames your body consumed, with oils and odors we your bones perfumed...

The Muslims in Pakistan have a wonderful belief about fragrance, stating that five hundred angels assemble when you die, and just before the attendants rub the body with scent, the angels sprinkle perfume brought from heaven. Essential oils were also well known for their use in the Egyptian culture to aid in the process of mummification, and to assist with the journey of the soul into the next world.

Once the soul has completely departed the body, it can then be washed and rubbed with anointing chrism, and saturated cotton can be placed inside all body orifices to prevent decay as the body is prepared for funeral or cremation. The body can then be dressed as appropriate to whatever ceremony has been decided upon.

Some final words...

There are an infinite variety of ways to use essential oils, and hopefully this book has made clear the many ways in which to use essential oils for a very ancient tool called anointing. Anointing is one of the greatest gifts I know to romance the Divine, to welcome and affect a grand evolution of Love in our hearts.

These ideas, concepts, beliefs, and choices are certainly not new, and it is only through the course of repeated use over the years, that experience has verified the power of anointing with sacred essential oils. My intention in writing this book has been to share the experiential knowledge learned through practice, with anyone who is seeking a deeper connection to God, Buddha, Brahman, Source, Great Spirit, Allah, or any other name for the Divine. There has yet to be a more powerful tool to use when looking to deepen our connection and the subsequent move into our Divine heritage than anointing. Nothing is more powerful for consecrating our selves as Divine emissaries of Love.

Our own mystical transformation is made possible by the grace given within the blessings of anointing with essential oils consecrated by the Divine, and our lives become nothing short of miraculous!

Bibliography

Ashely-Farrand, Thomas
  Healing Mantras, Ballantine Wellspring, New York NY 1999

Bravo, Brett
  Crystal Healing Secrets, Warner Books, New York NY 1988

Cunningham, Scott
  Magical Aromatherapy, Llewellyn Publications, St. Paul MN 1994

Hall, Judy
  The Crystal Bible, Godsfield Press, Hampshire UK 2003

Harkness, Peter
  Roses, Harry Abrams, Inc., New York NY 2005

Holy Bible, King James Version

Lad, Dr. Vasant
  Ayurveda - The Science of Self-Healing, Lotus Press,
    Twin Lakes WI 2004

LaVabre, Marcel
  Aromatherapy Workbook, Thorsons, Hammersmith UK 1993

Lawless, Julia
  The Illustrated Encyclopedia of Essential Oils, Element Books,
    Rockport MA 1995

Meadows, Kenneth
  Earth Medicine, Element Books, Rockport,MA 1991

Melody
  Love is in the Earth, Earth Love Publishing, CO 1995

Olfactory Research Fund
  Compendium of Olfactory Research, Kendall Publishing, New York NY 1995

Oslie, Pamala
  Life Colors, New World Library, Novato CA 2000
  Love Colors, New World Library, Novato CA 2007

Price, Shirley
  Aromatherapy for Common Ailments, Fireside, New York NY 1991
  Aromatherapy Workbook, Healing Arts Press, Rochester VT 1993

Ryman, Danielle
Aromatherapy, Bantam Books, New York NY 1991

Raphaell, Katrina
Crystal Healing Vol. 1, 2 & 3, Aurora Press, Santa Fe NM 1987

Schnaubelt, Kurt
Advanced Aromatherapy, Healing Arts Press, Rochester VT 1998

Sommerard, Michel
Le Chemin Des Aromes, Non Nobis, France 1990

Sun Bear, Wabun Wind, Chrysalis Mulligan
Dancing with the Wheel, Fireside, New York NY 1991

Tisserand, Maggie
Essence of Love, Harper Collins, New York NY 1993

Walker, Barbara
The Book of Sacred Stones, Harper, San Francisco CA 1989

Wildwood, Chrissie
Erotic Aromatherapy, Sterling, San Francisco CA 1989

Worwood, Valerie Ann
The Complete Book of Essential Oils and Aromatherapy, New World
Library, Novato CA 1991
The Fragrant Mind, New World Library, Novato CA 1996
The Fragrant Heavens, New World Library, Novato CA 1999

Young, Gary
Aromatherapy, The Essential Beginning, Essential Press Publishing,
Salt Lake City UT 1995

About the Author

Allison Stillman is a teacher, visionary, holistic practitioner, and ordained minister. She travels extensively teaching workshops on the art of anointing, and sharing her love and knowledge of essential oils. Once practiced throughout the ancient world, Allison has reclaimed anointing and combined its divine secrets with modern research, bringing a new awareness to a sacred art.

The Sacred Art of Anointing is her first book and was over twenty years in the making. After witnessing scores of miraculous experiences with her clients, she was guided to share the art of anointing with the world in the hope that more people will be inspired to apply consecrated essential oils as a tool for awakening higher consciousness.

Allison lives in Ojai, CA with her husband Michael, and her temple cat Mr. Wiskers. Her private aromatic practice includes individual anointing ceremonies for clients from around the world, as well as custom blending signature HeartScent anointing oils.

Please visit her website: www.romancingthedivine.com

Made in the USA
Middletown, DE
04 October 2016